Numbers 0-20 Flash Card Booklet©

With Ten-Frames

By Schoolhouse Heaven™

www.schoolhouseheaven.com

Goose Creek, SC

Copyright © 2016 Schoolhouse Heaven All Rights Reserved

Table of Contents

Counting 1-10	4
Learning 0-10	15
Counting 11-20	38
Learning 11-20	49
Counting 1-20	70
Ten-frame 0-10	91
Ten-frame 11-20	115

First, let's practice counting 1-10.

2

3

4

5

6

7

8

q

10

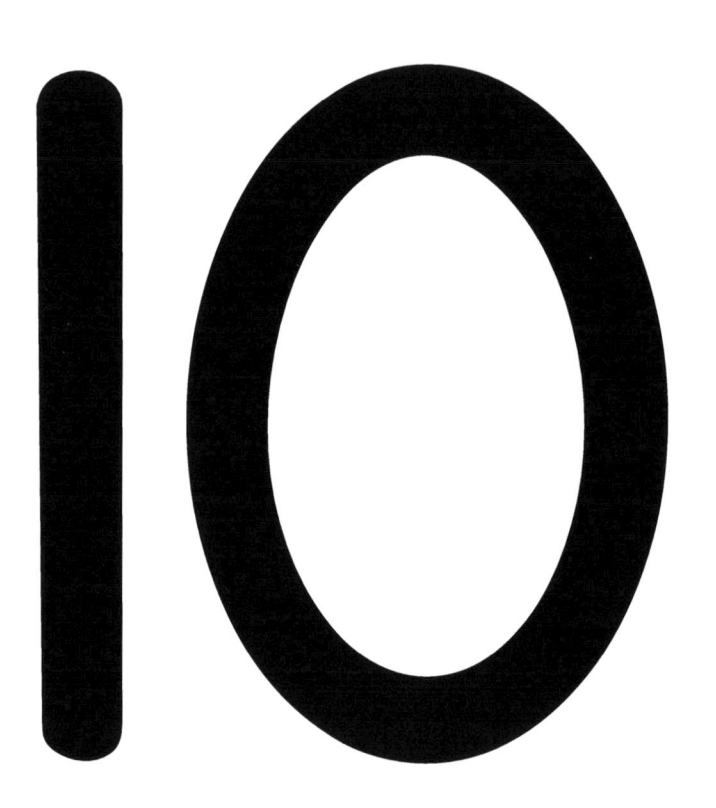

Great job! Now let's go over numbers 0-10.

0

Can you hold up zero fingers?

There are zero counters in the ten-frame.

1

Can you hold up one finger?

There is one counter in the ten-frame.

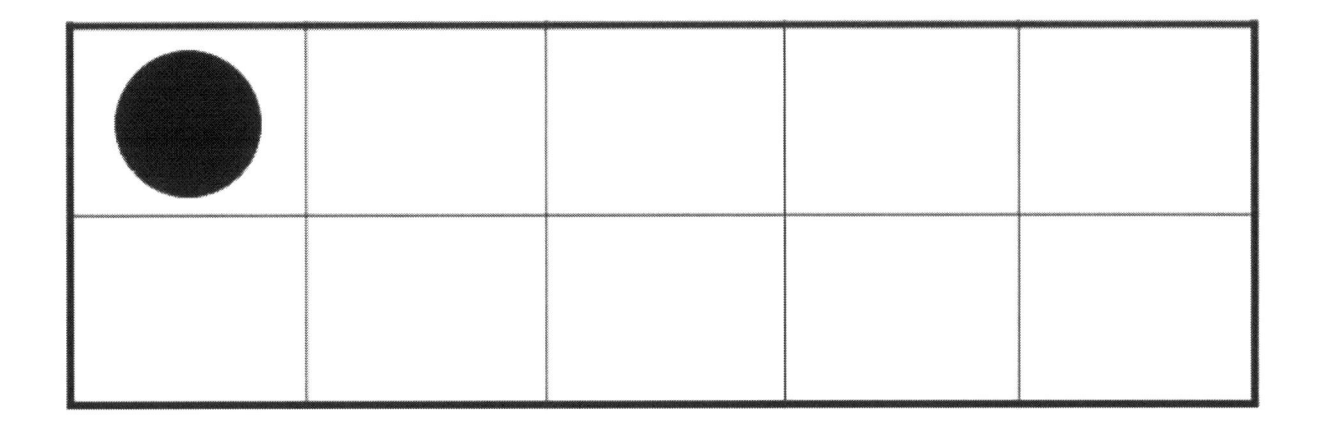

2

Can you hold up two fingers?

There are two counters in the ten-frame.

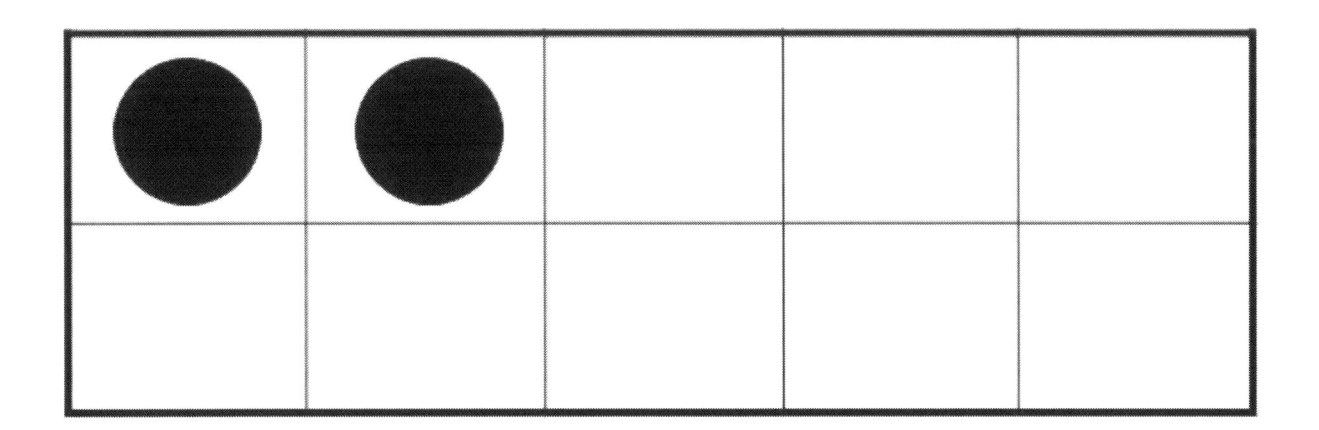

3

Can you hold up three fingers?

There are three counters in the ten-frame.

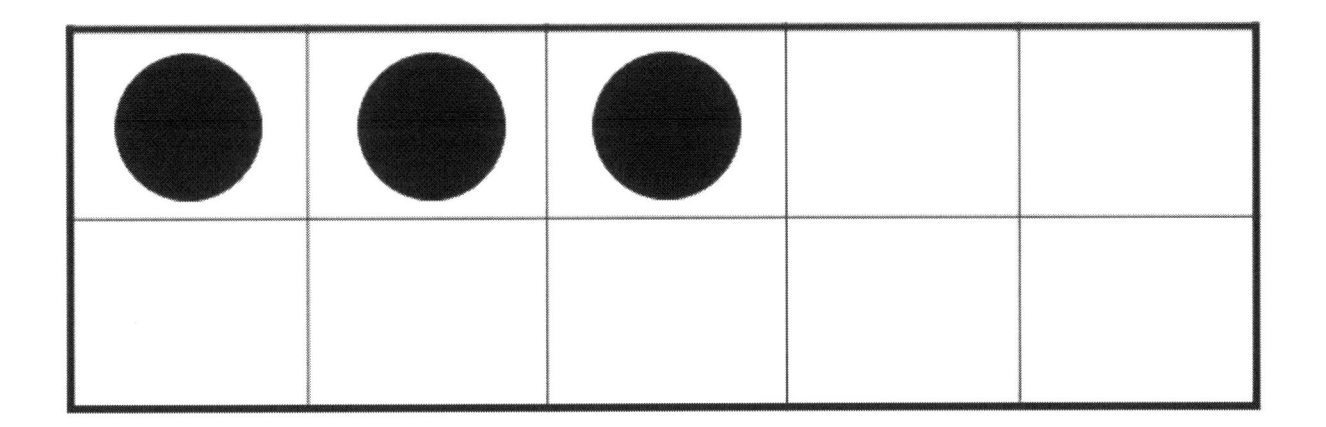

4

Can you hold up four fingers?

There are four counters in the ten-frame.

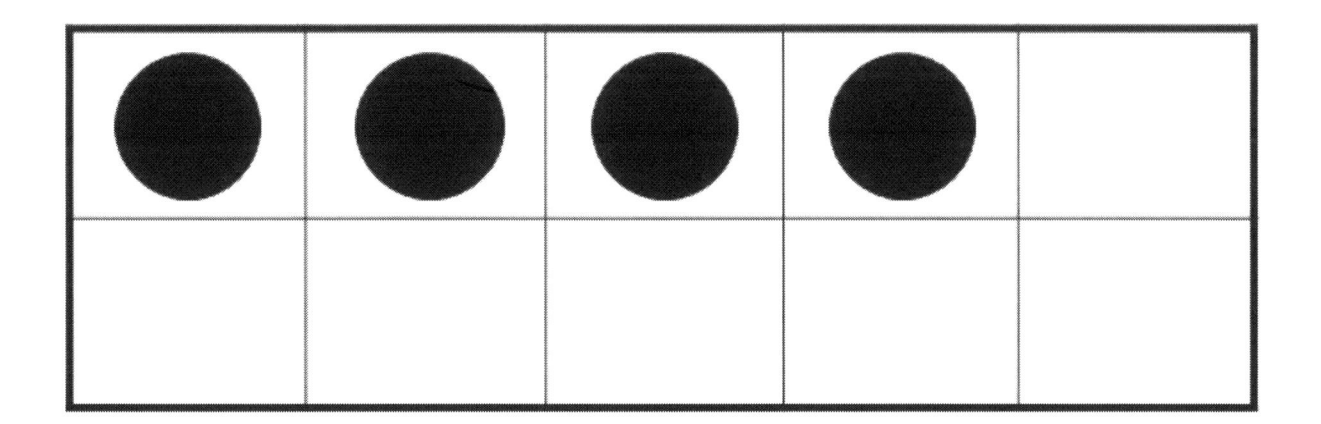

5

Can you hold up five fingers?

There are five counters in the ten-frame.

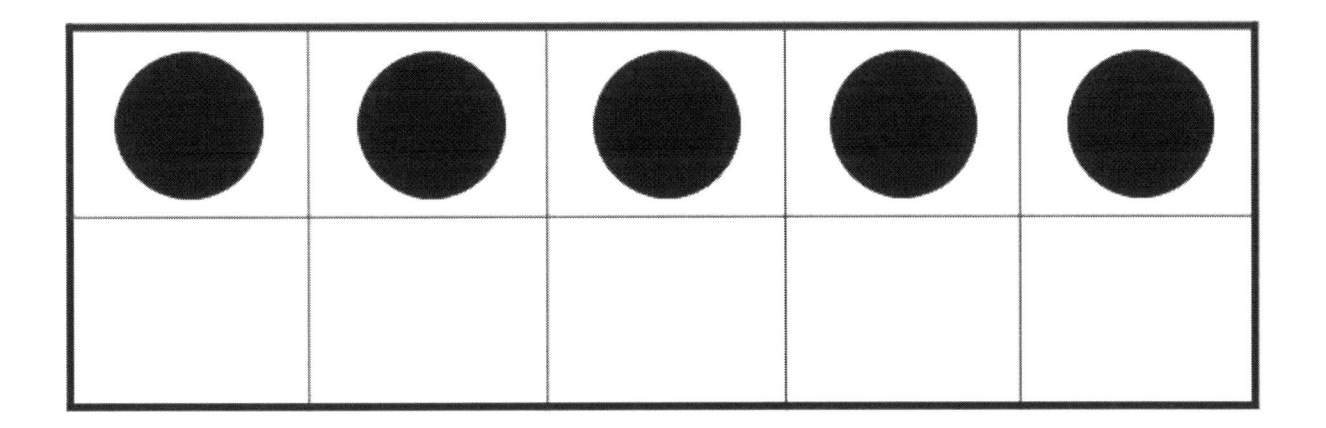

6

Can you hold up six fingers?

There are six counters in the ten-frame.

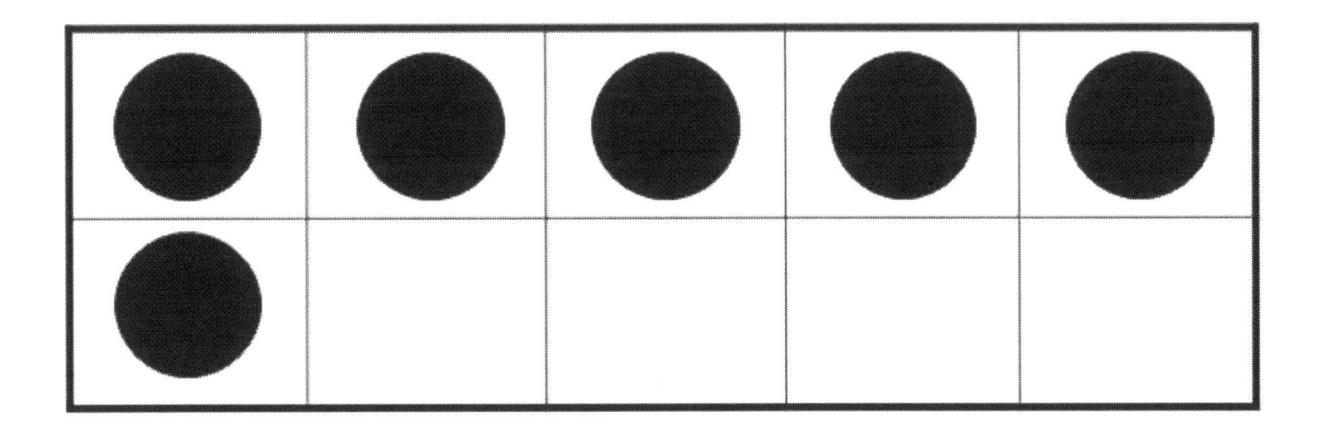

7

Can you hold up seven fingers?

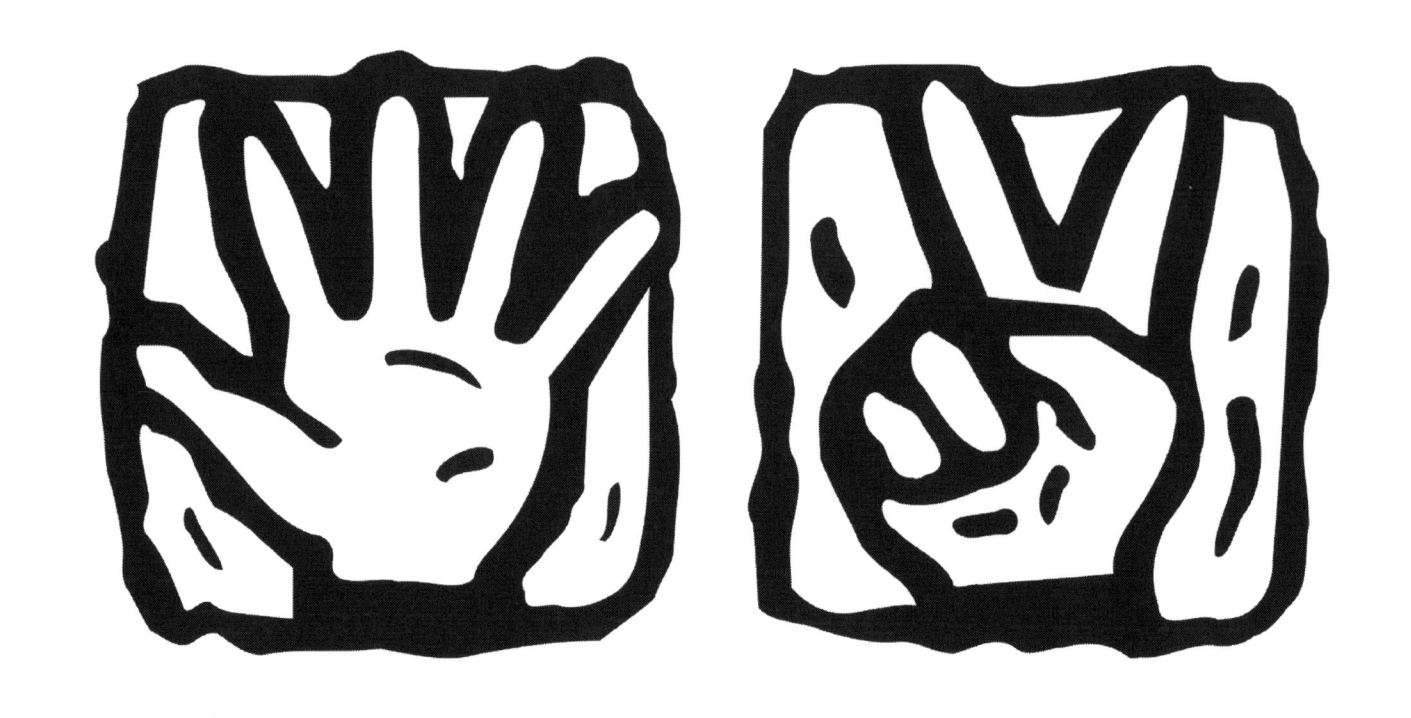

There are seven counters in the ten-frame.

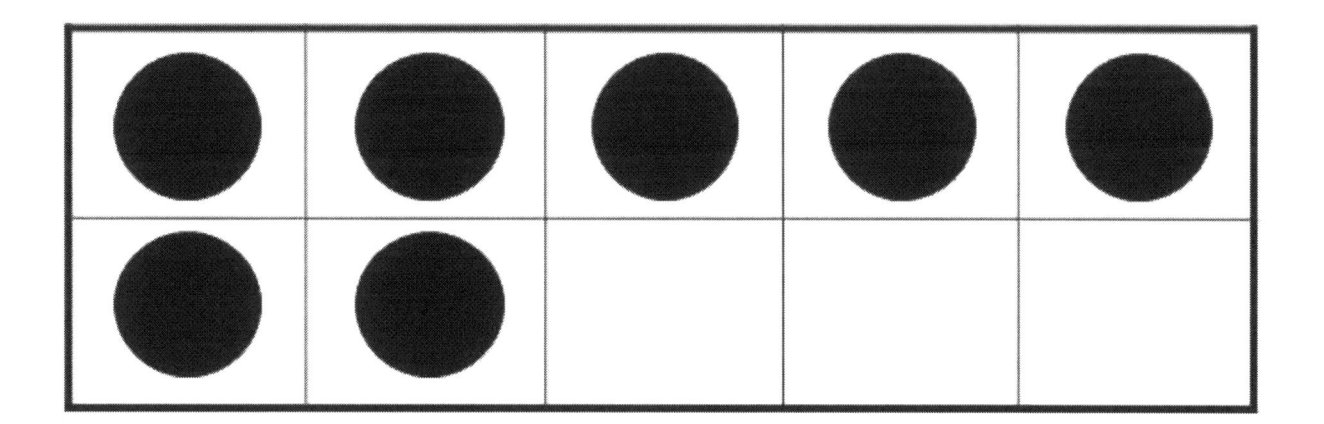

8

Can you hold up eight fingers?

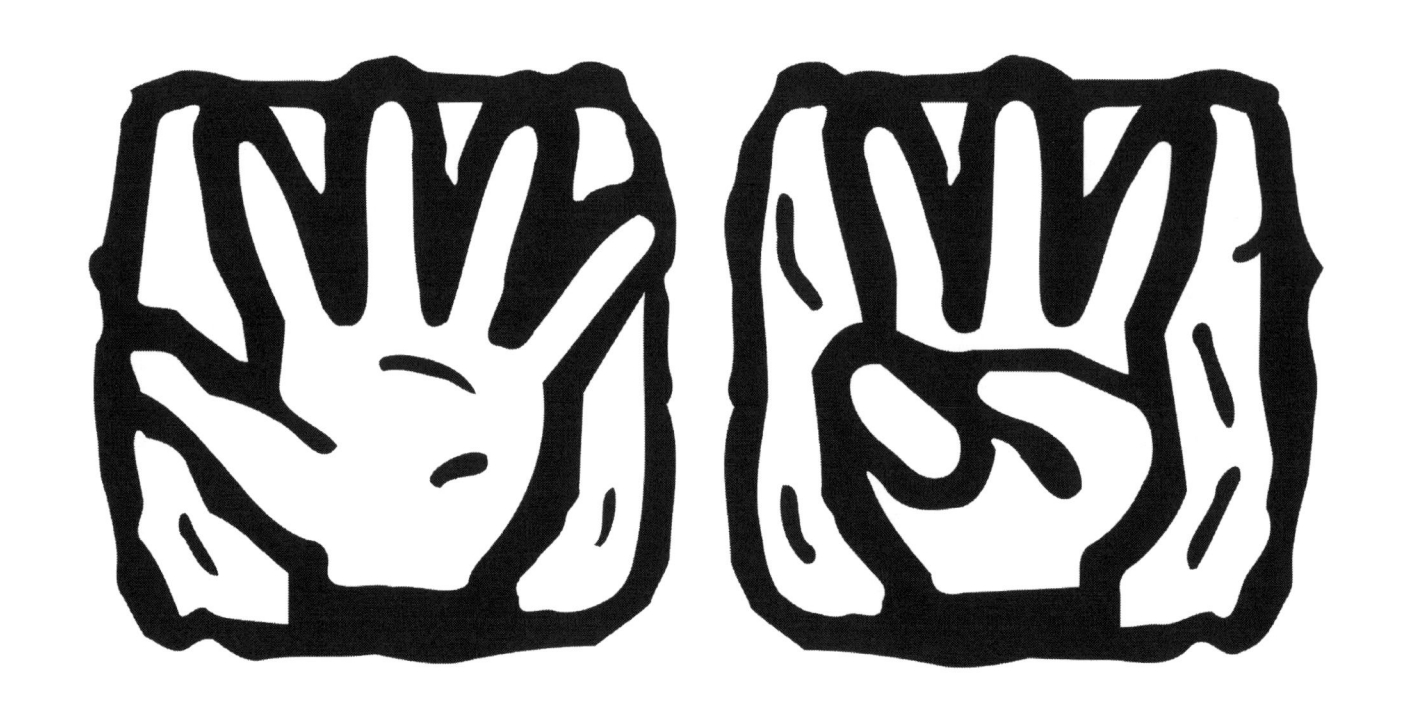

There are eight counters in the ten-frame.

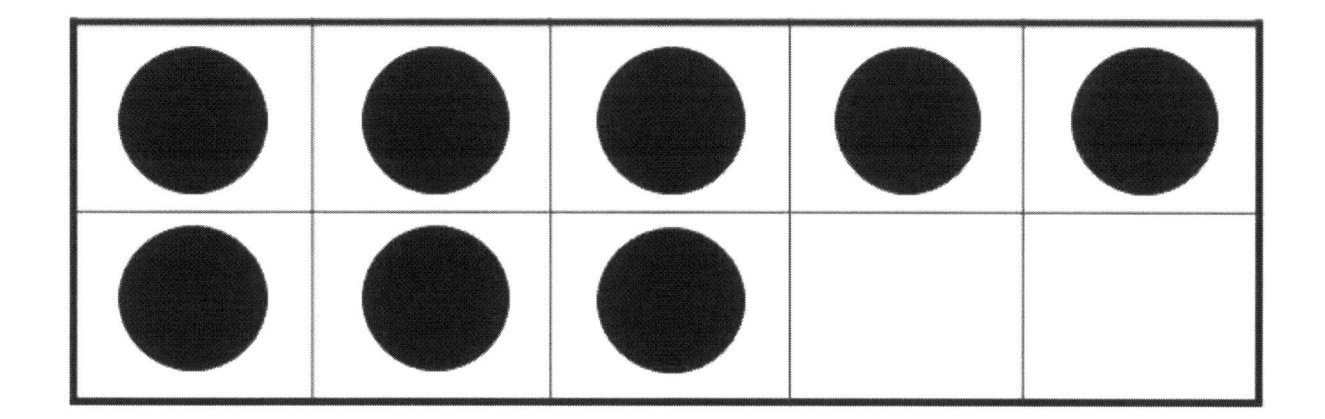

q

Can you hold up nine fingers?

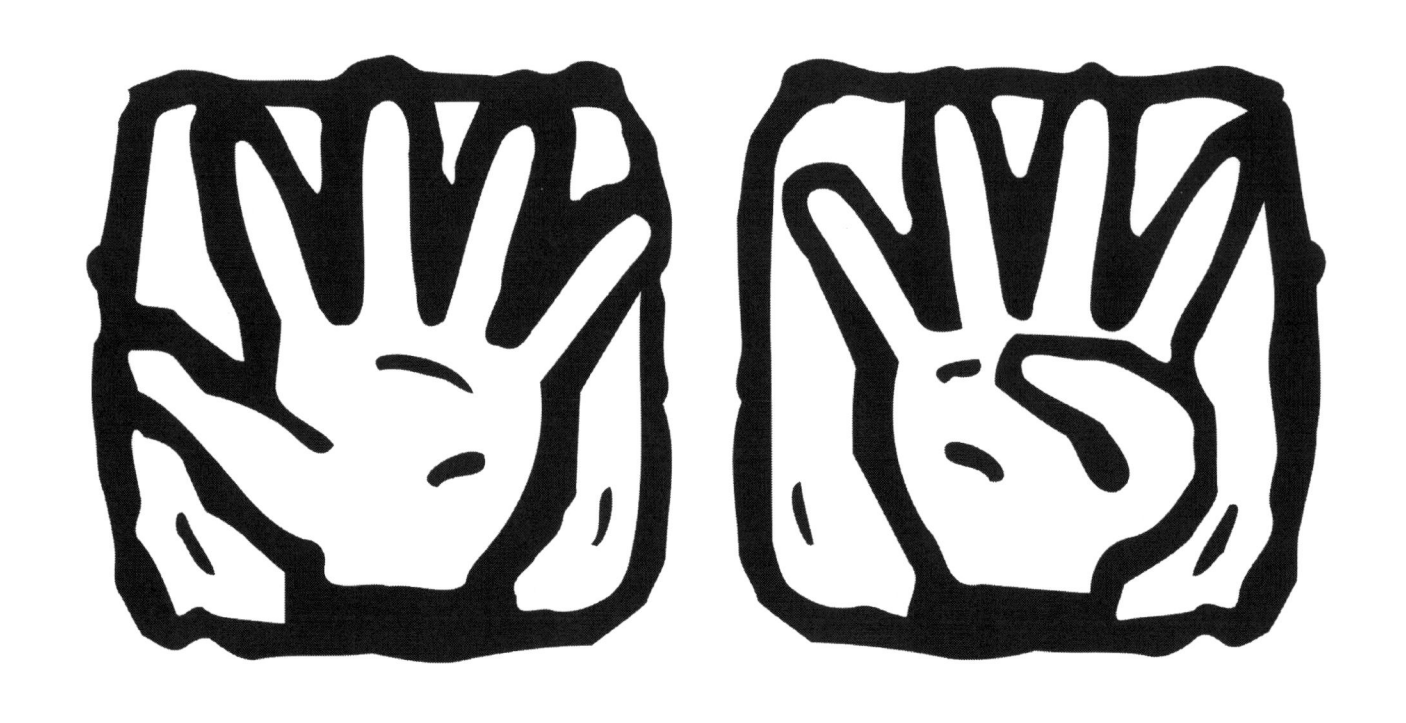

There are nine counters in the ten-frame.

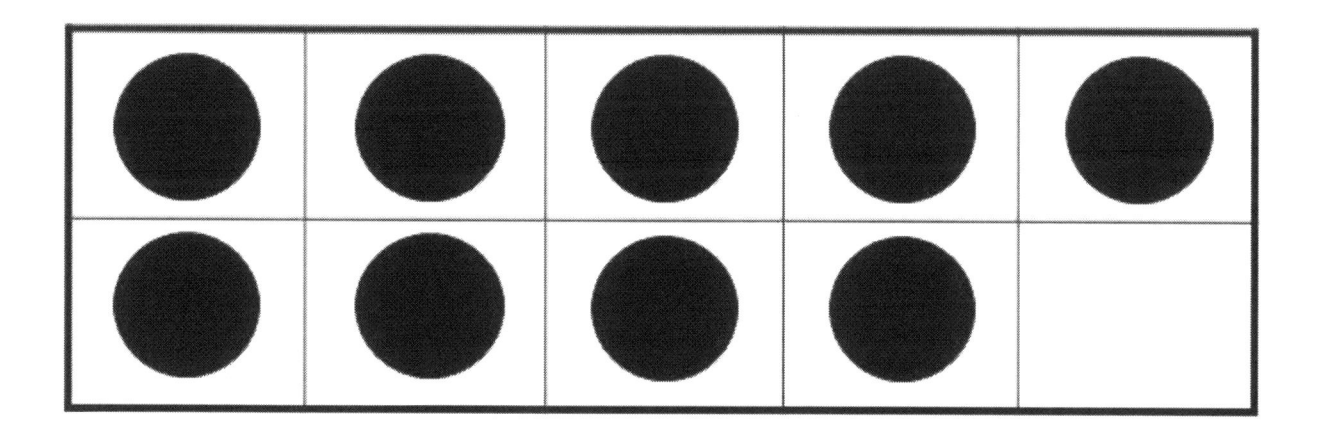

10

Can you hold up ten fingers?

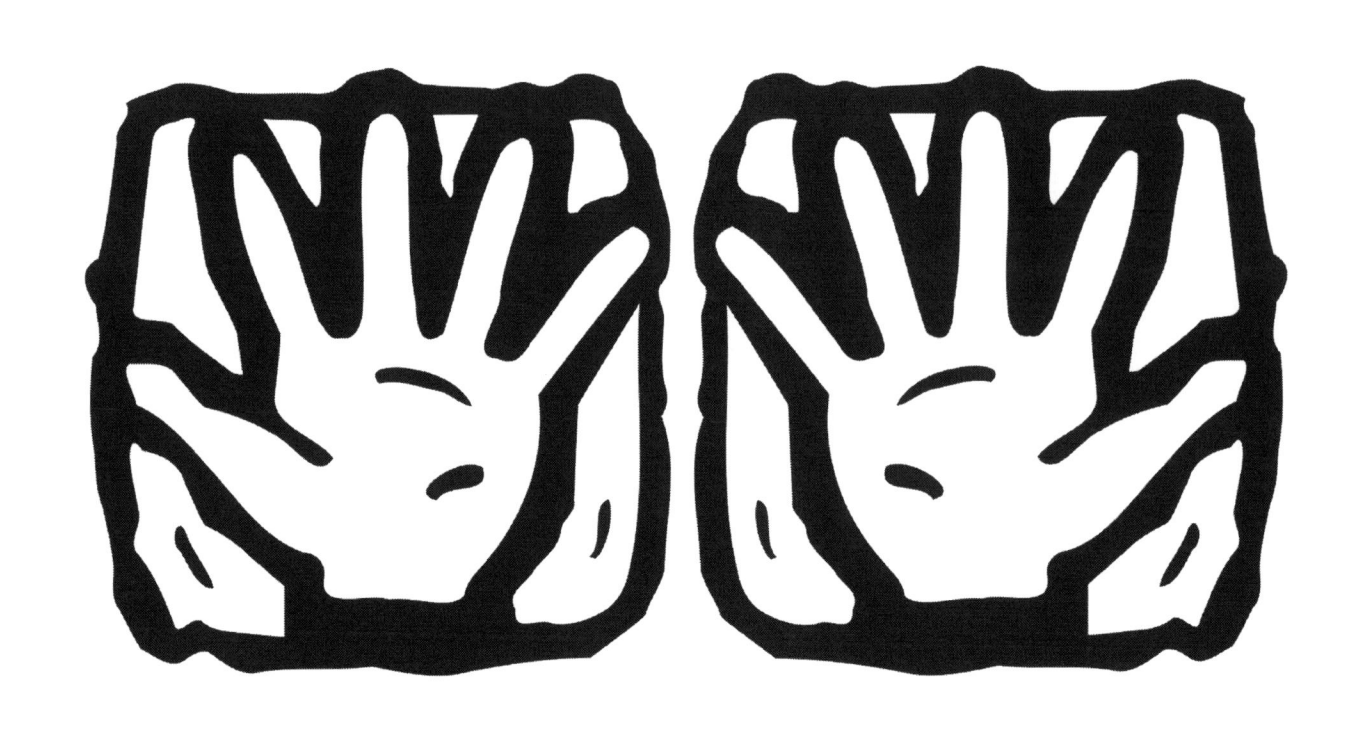

There are ten counters in the ten-frame.

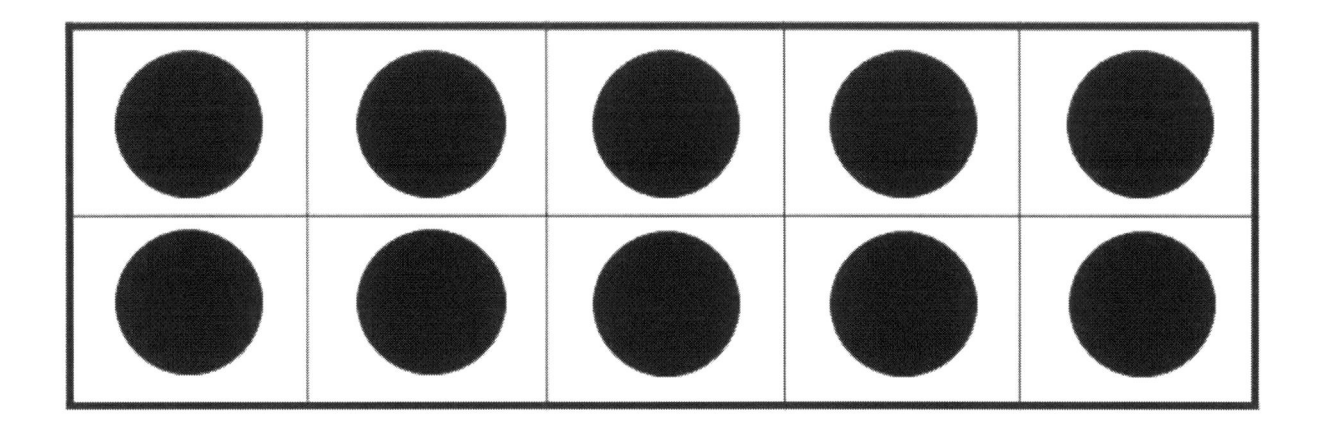

Now let's practice counting 11-20.

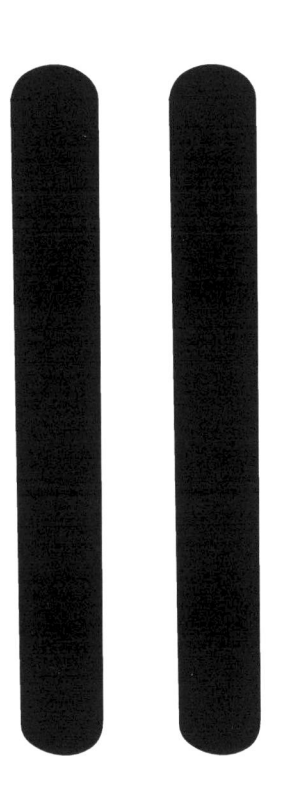

12

13

14

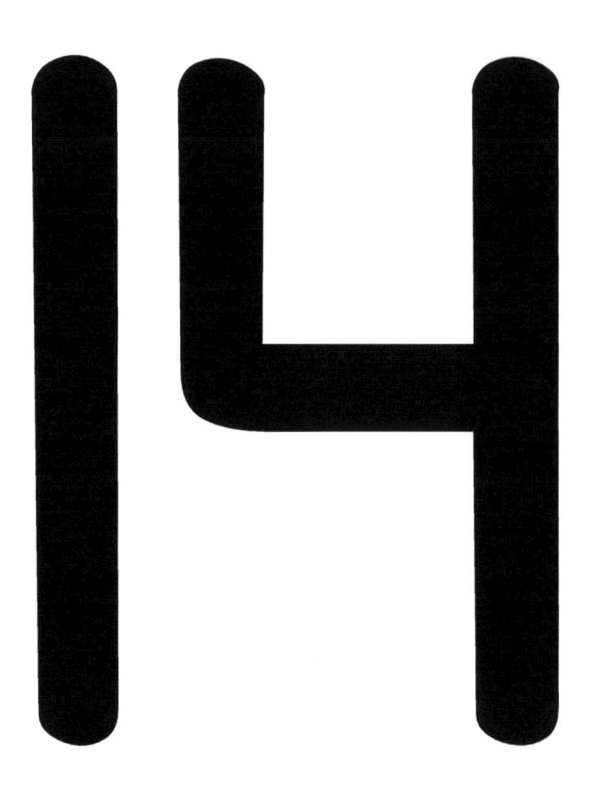

15

16

17

18

19

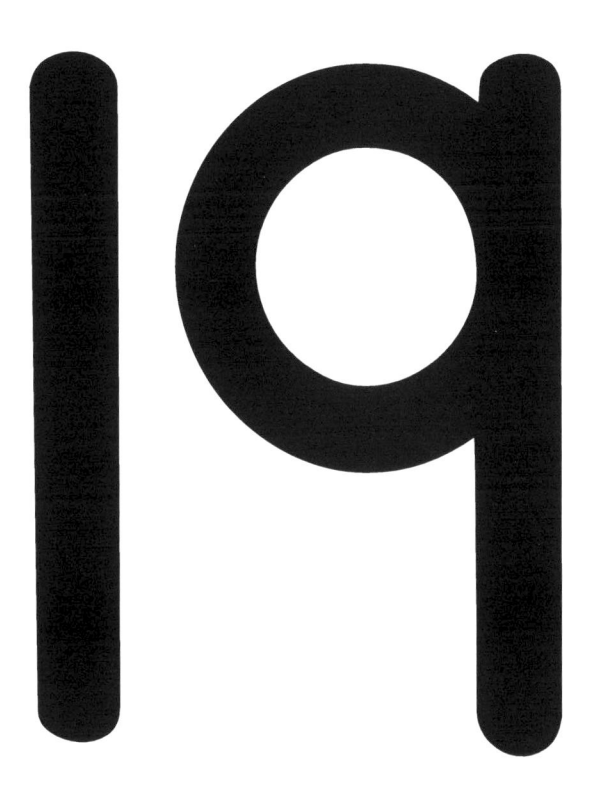

20

Great job! Now let's go over numbers 11-20.

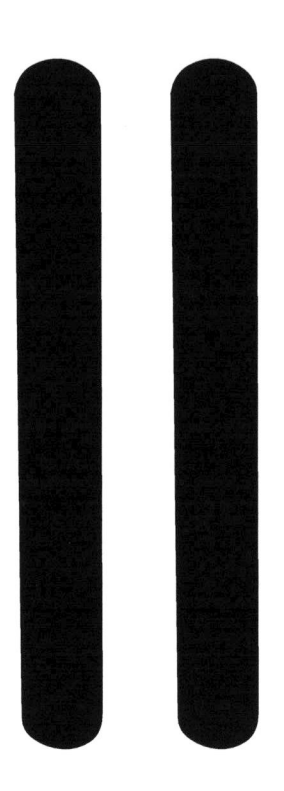

There are eleven counters in the ten-frames. Touch each one and count.

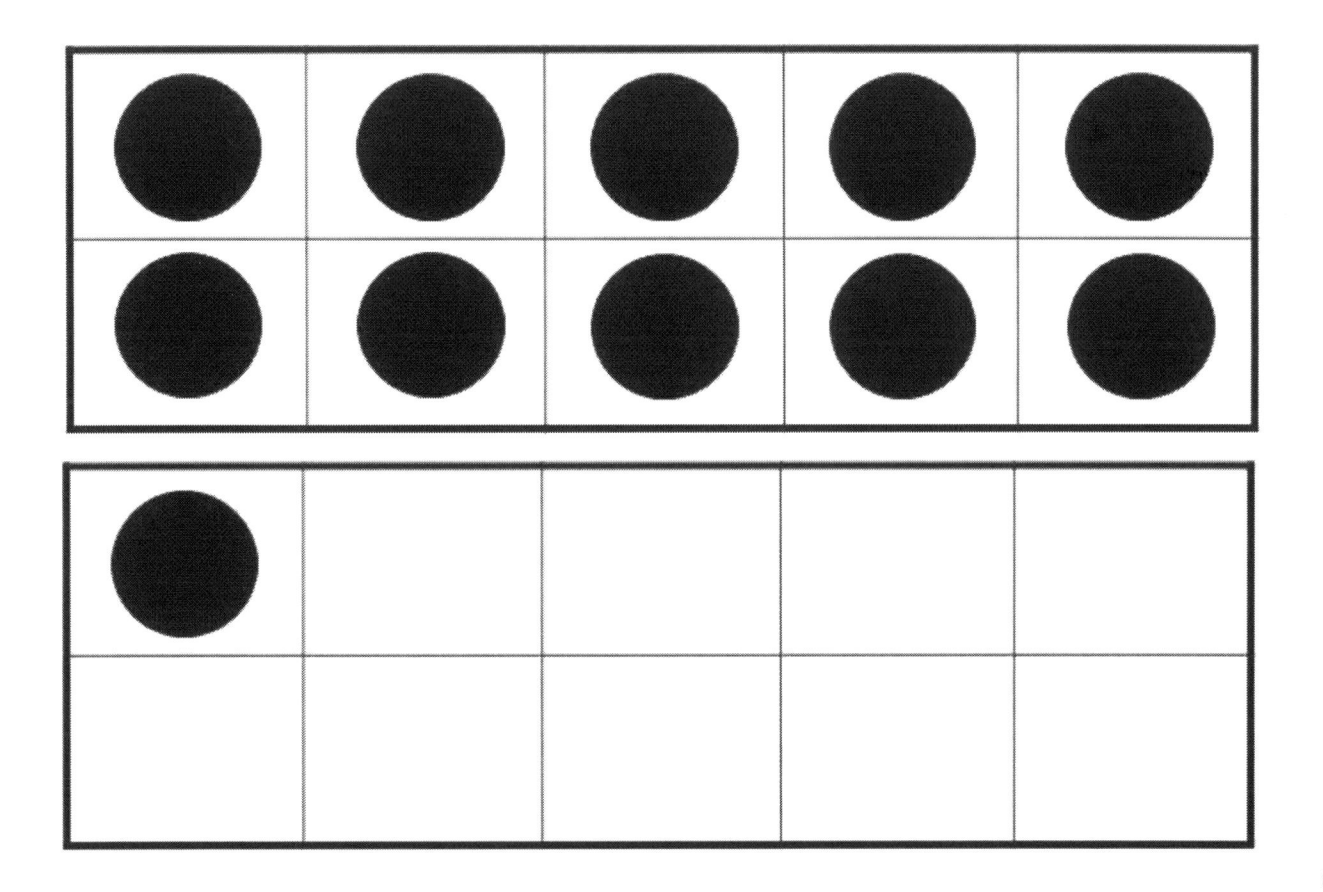

12

There are twelve counters in the ten-frames. Touch each one and count.

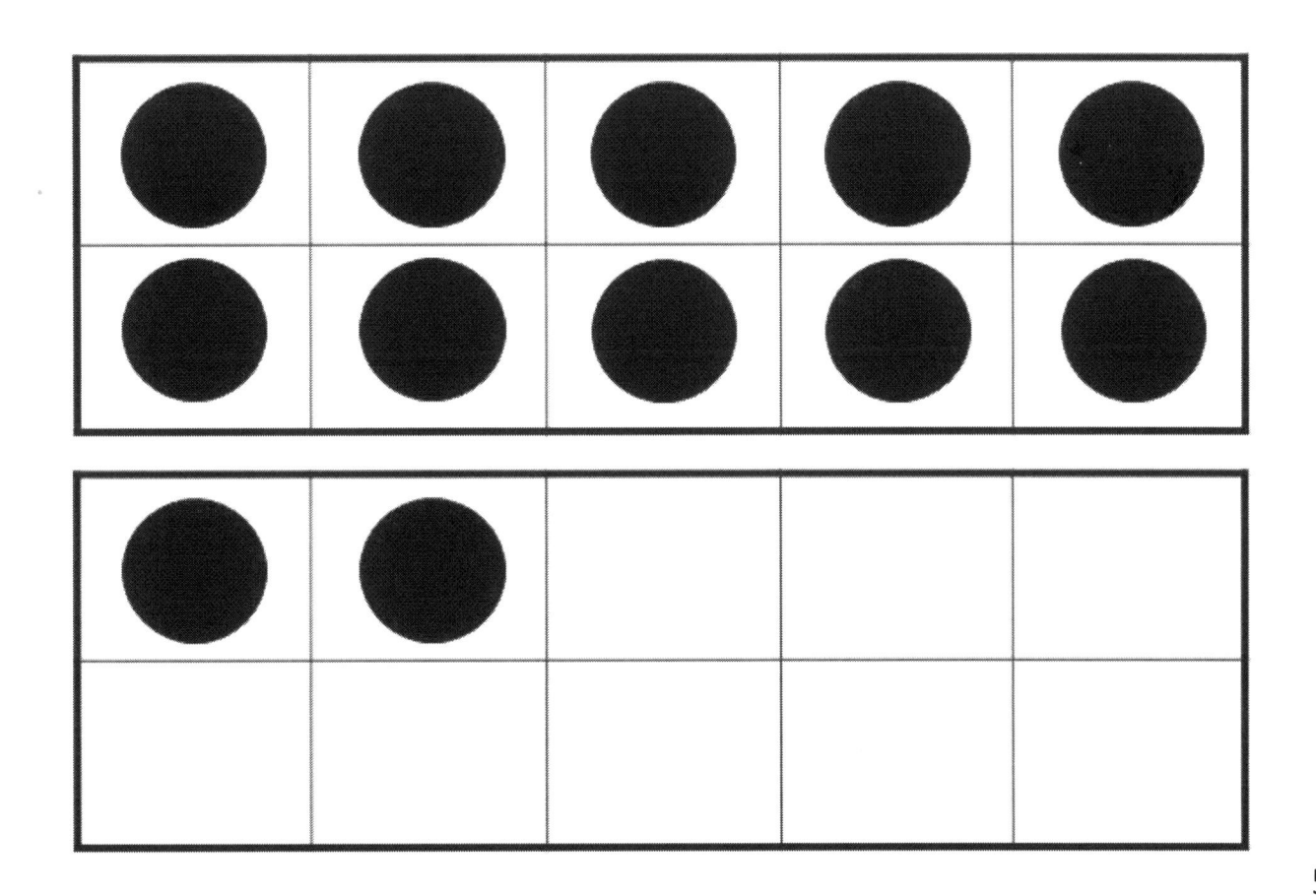

13

There are thirteen counters in the ten-frames. Touch each one and count.

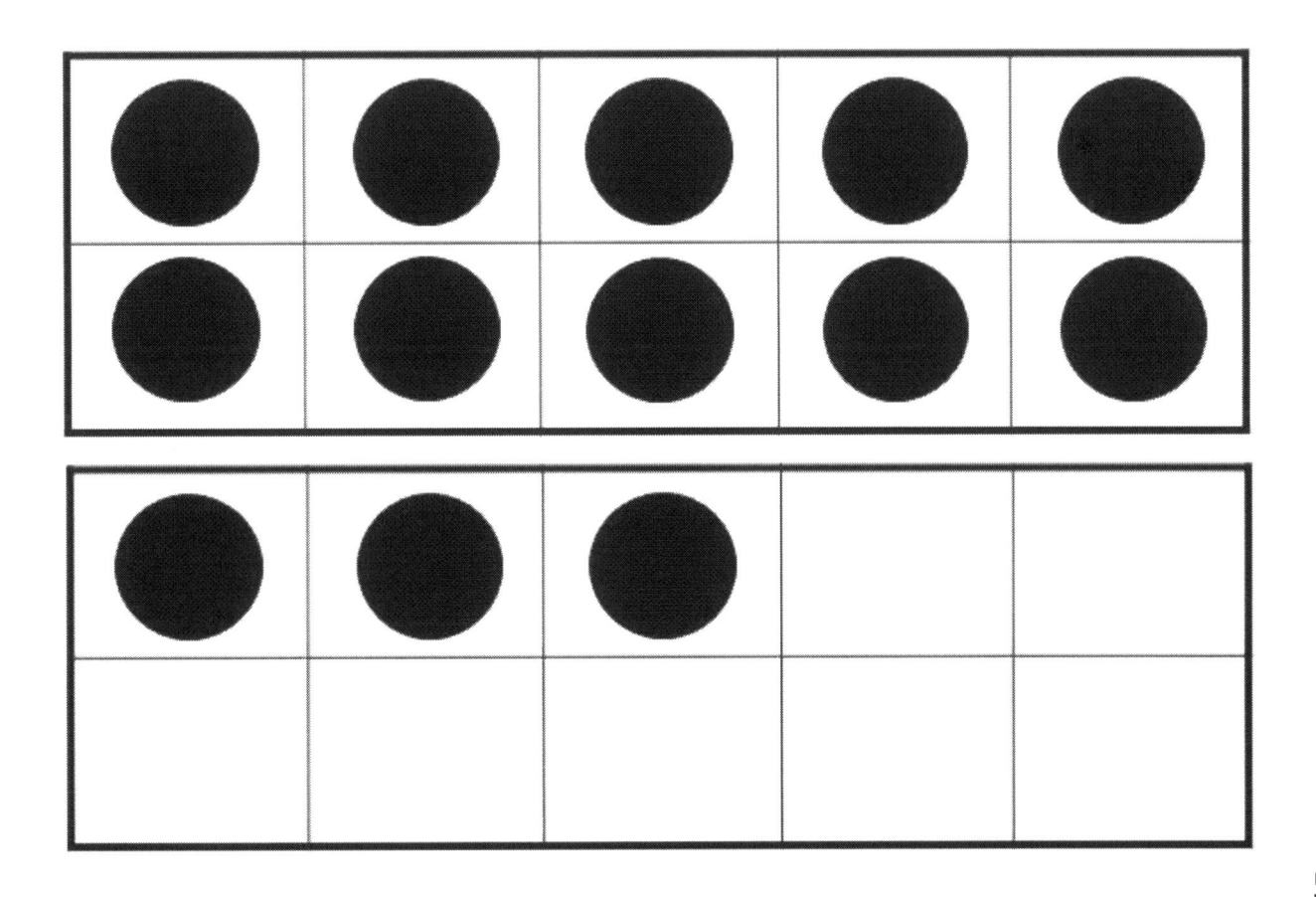

14

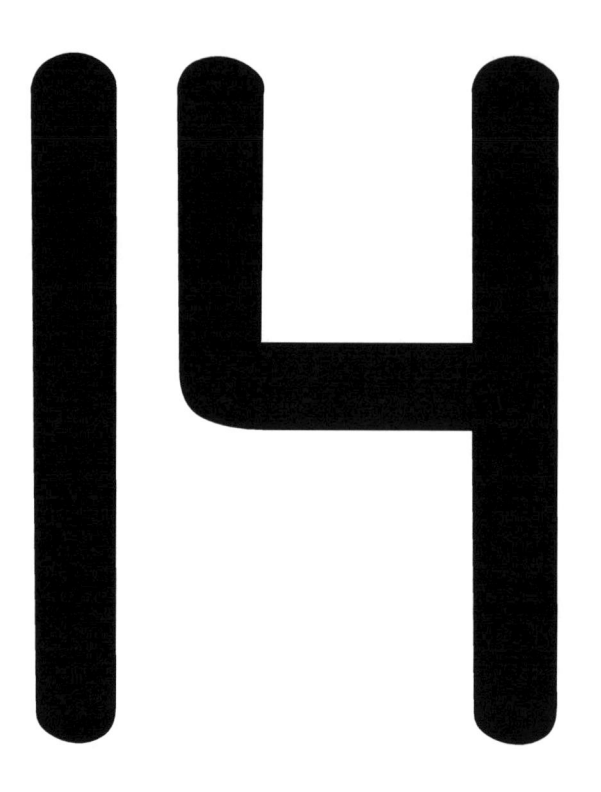

There are fourteen counters in the ten-frames. Touch each one and count.

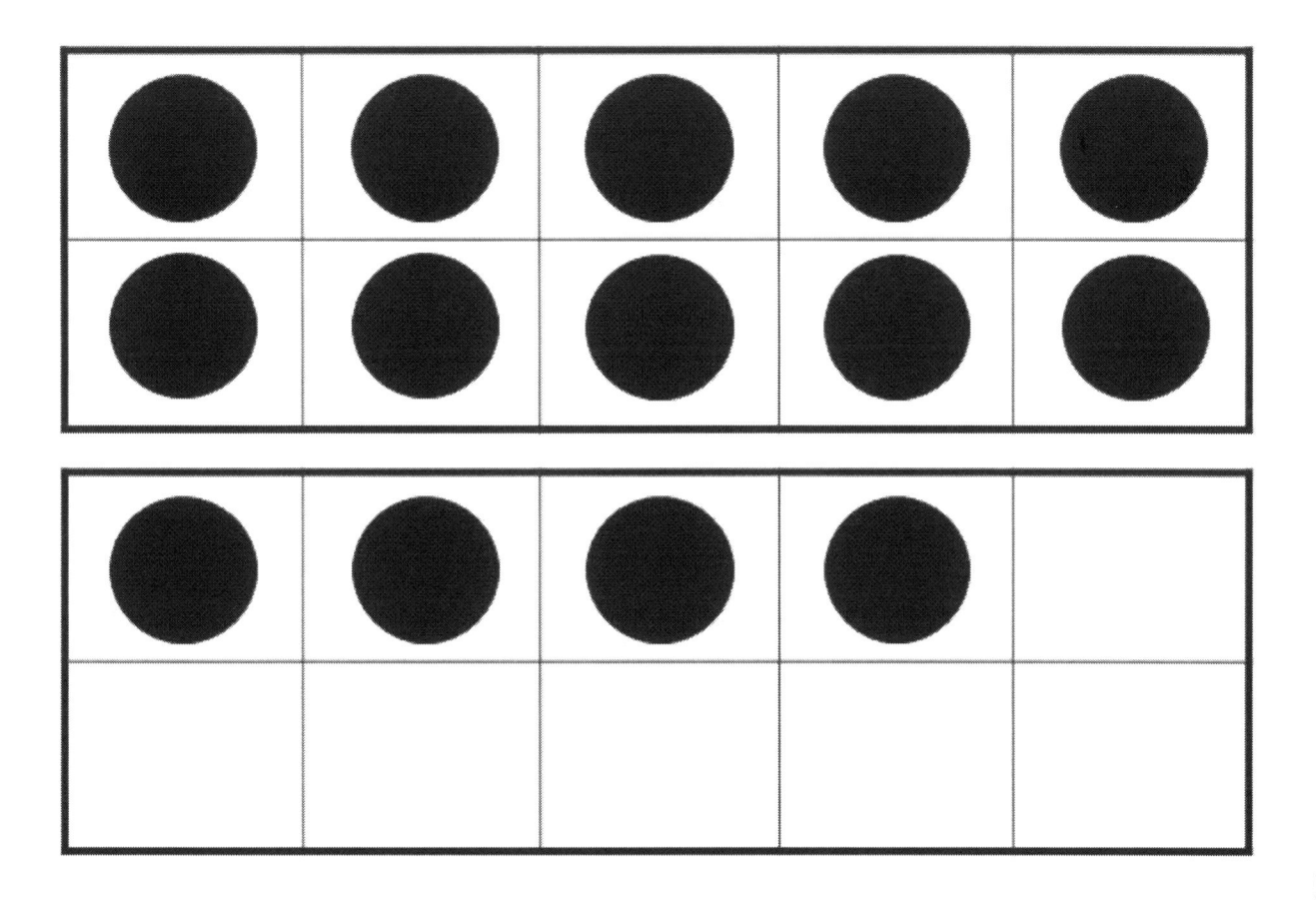

15

There are fifteen counters in the ten-frames. Touch each one and count.

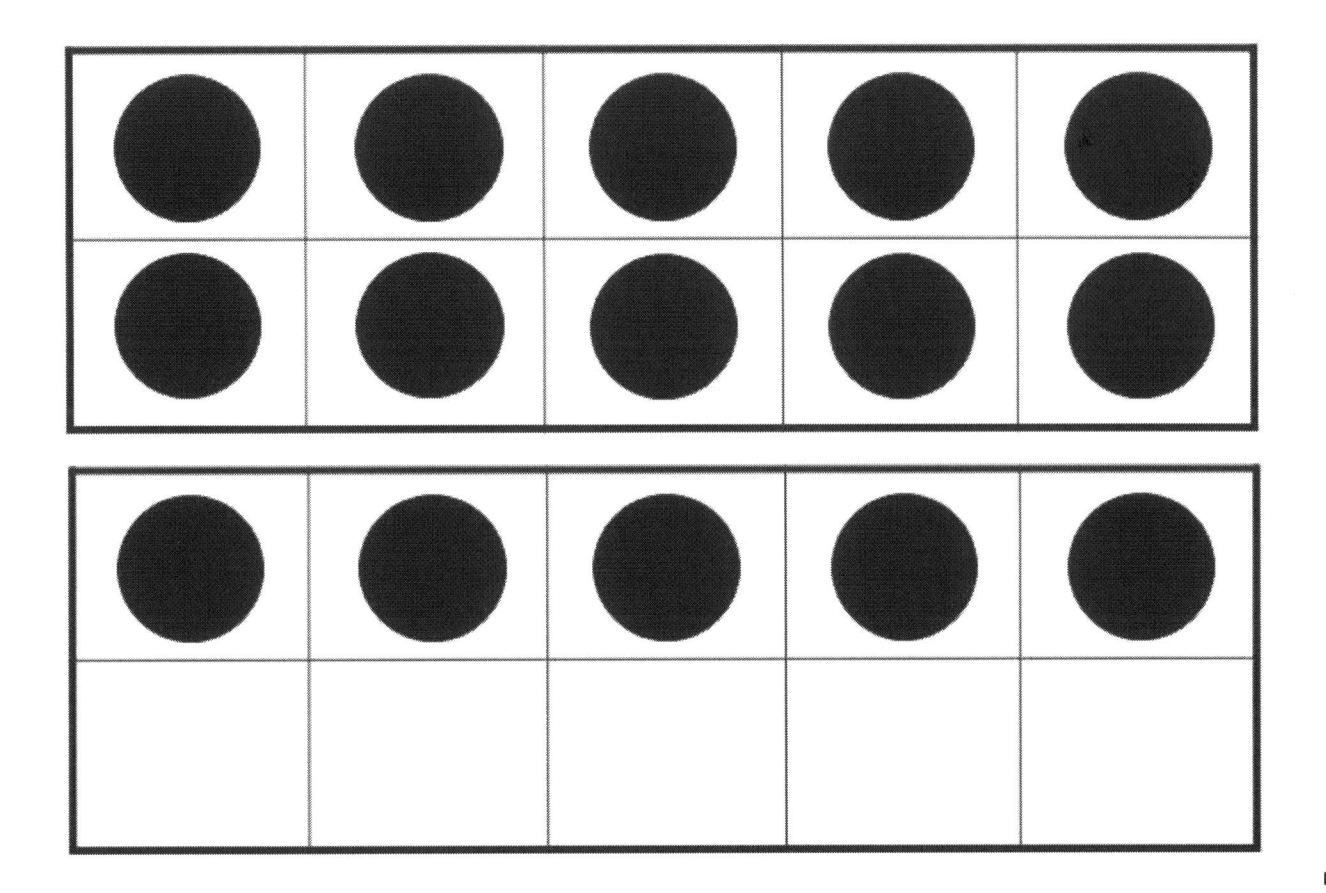

16

There are sixteen counters in the ten-frames. Touch each one and count.

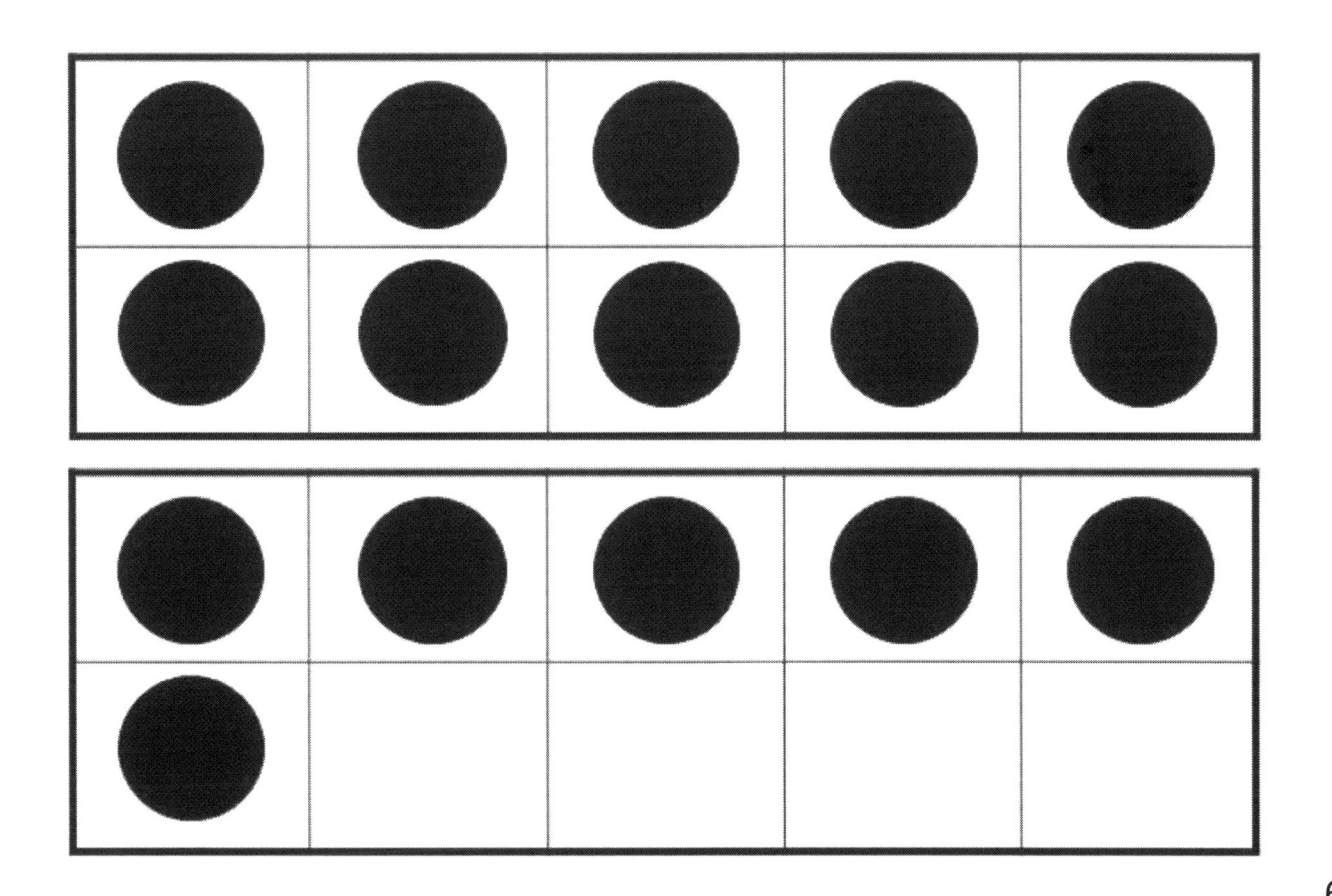

17

There are seventeen counters in the ten-frames. Touch each one and count.

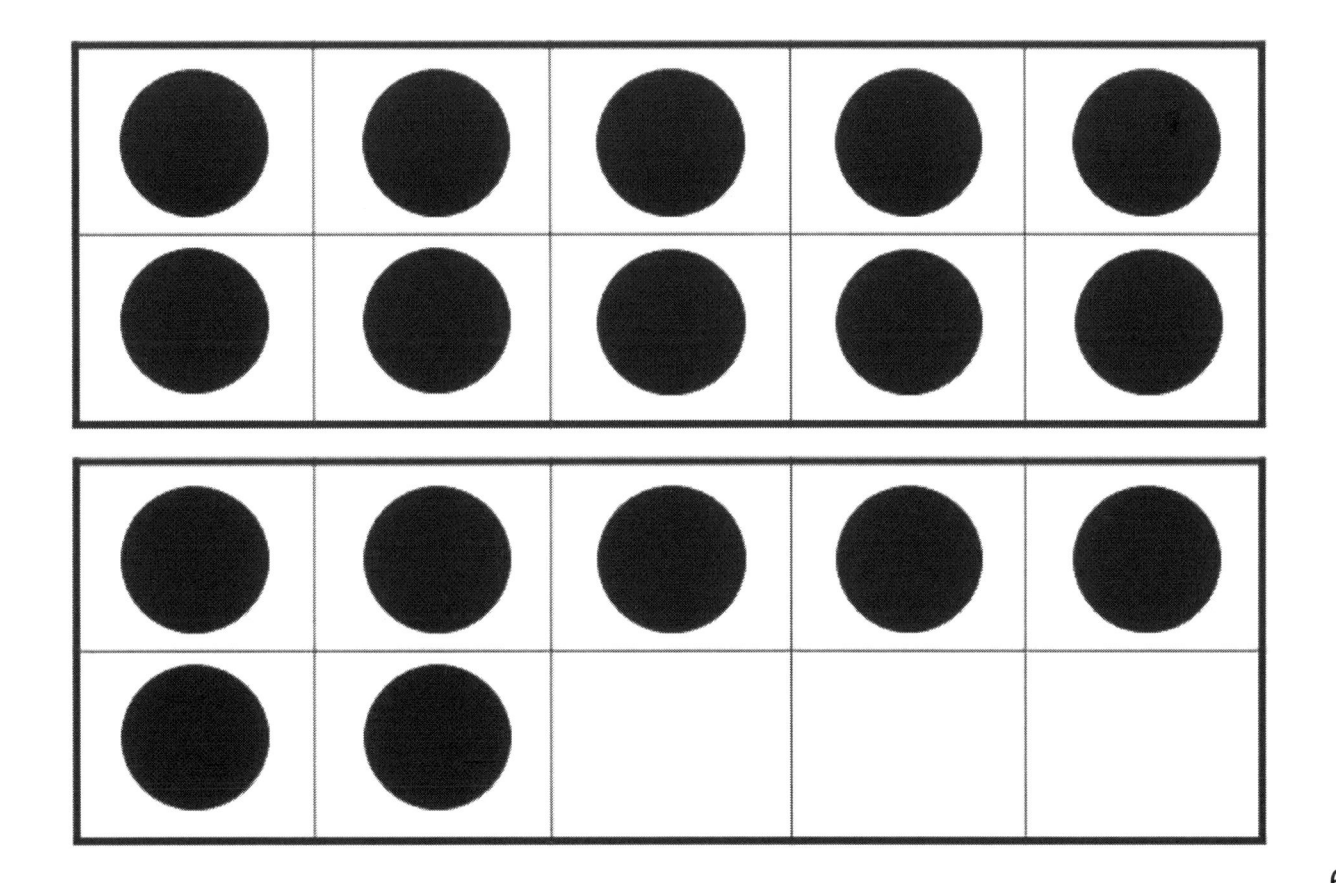

18

There are eighteen counters in the ten-frames. Touch each one and count.

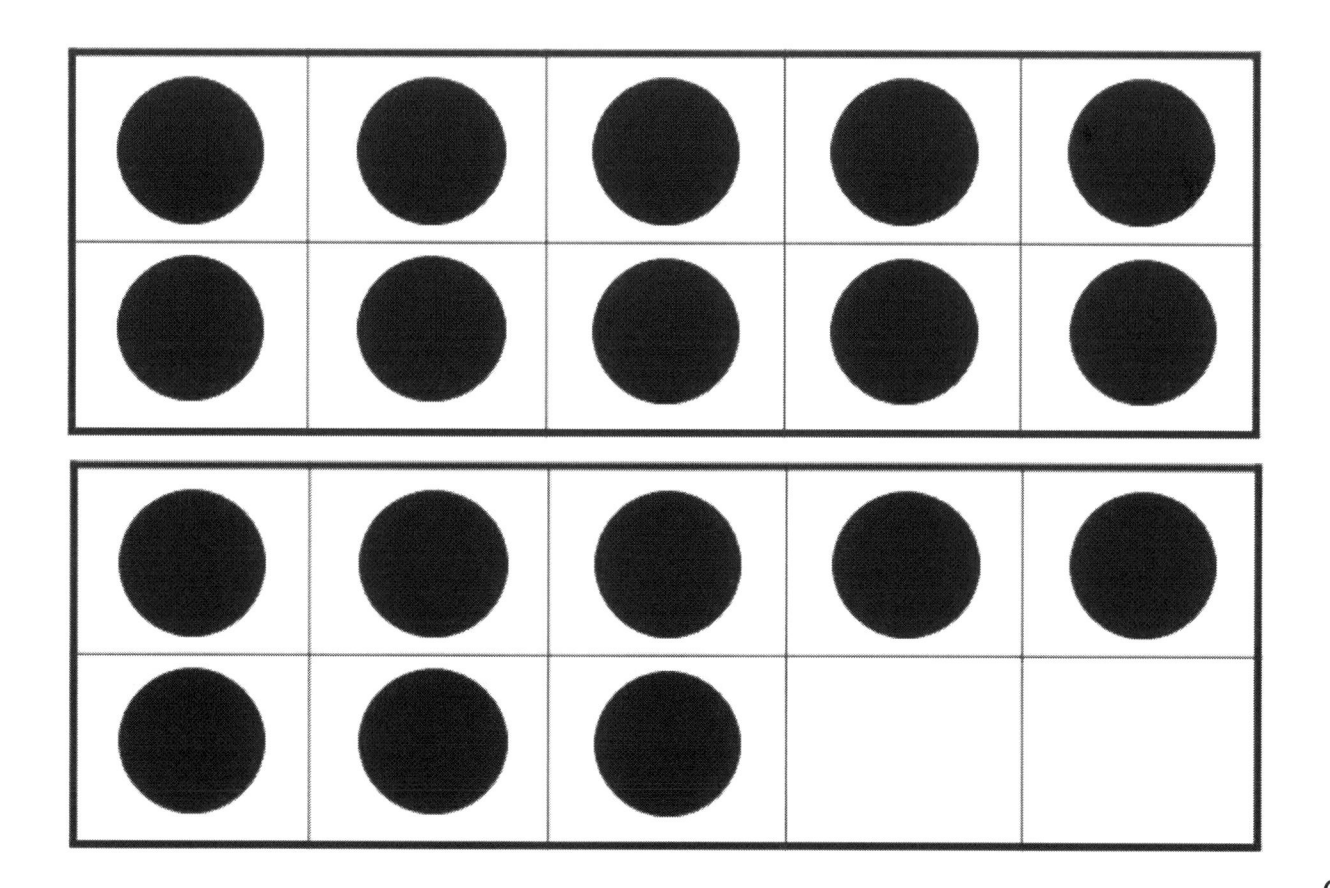

19

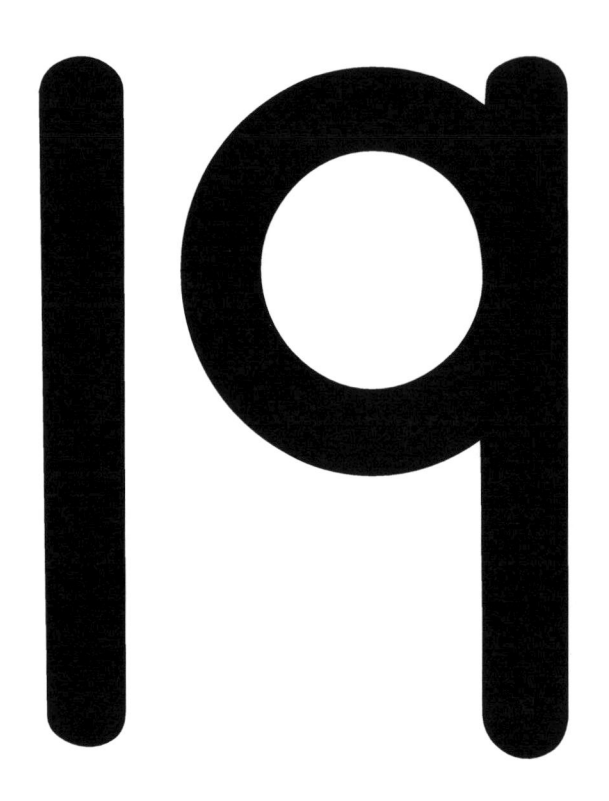

There are nineteen counters in the ten-frames. Touch each one and count.

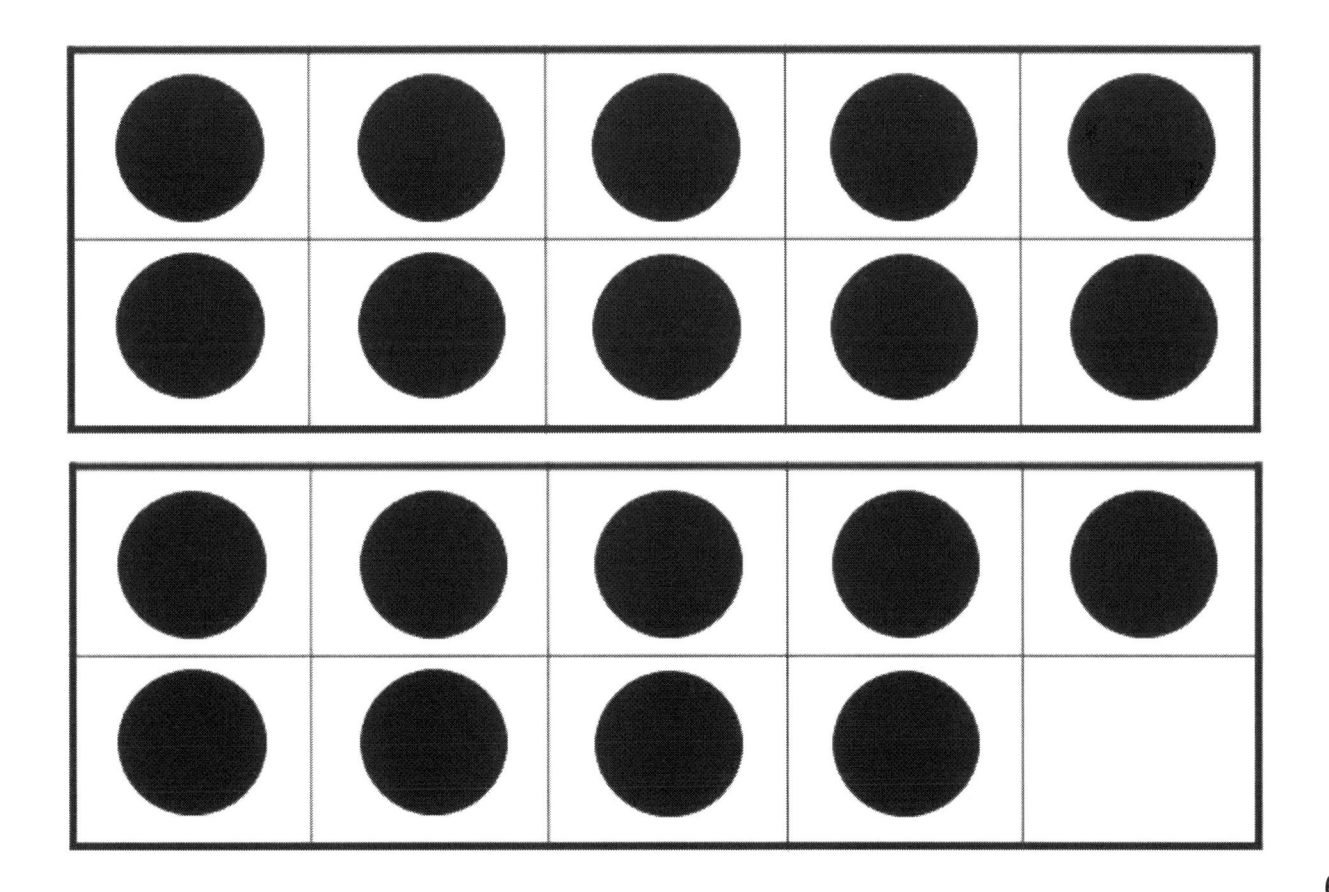

20

There are twenty counters in the ten-frames. Touch each one and count.

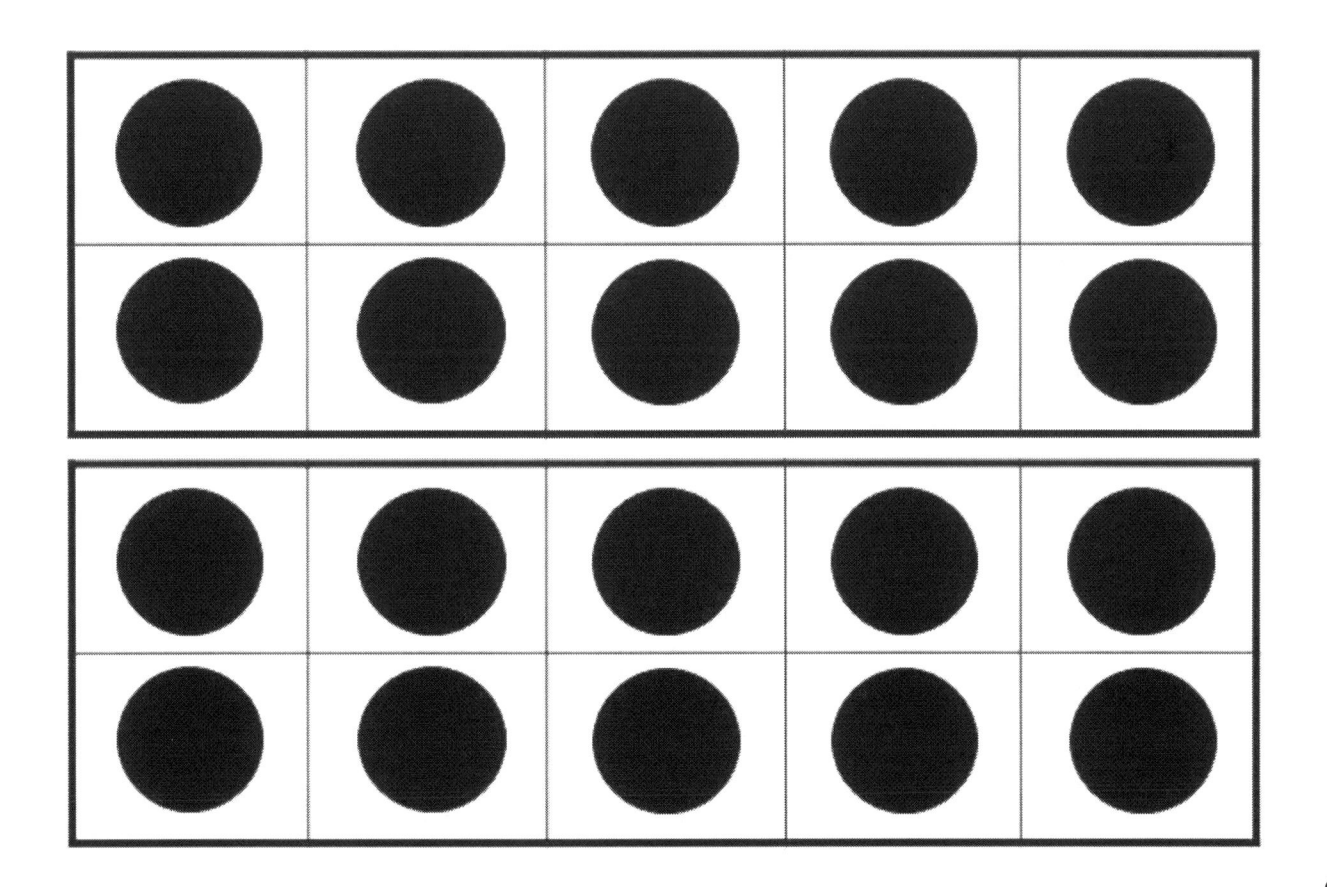

Now let's count 1-20.

2

3

ч

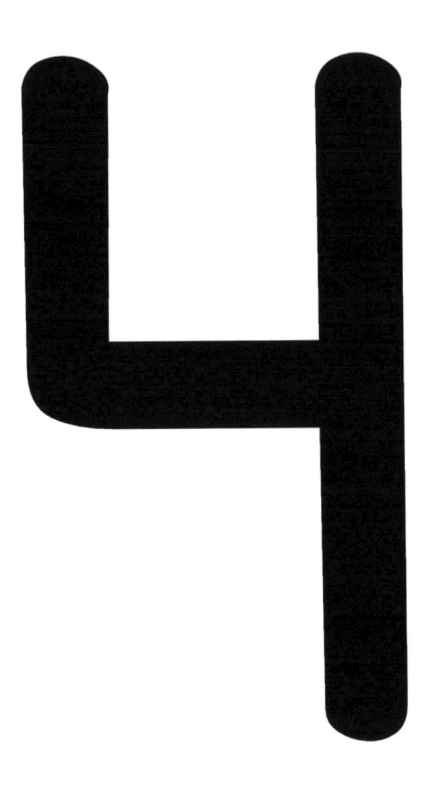

5

6

7

8

q

10

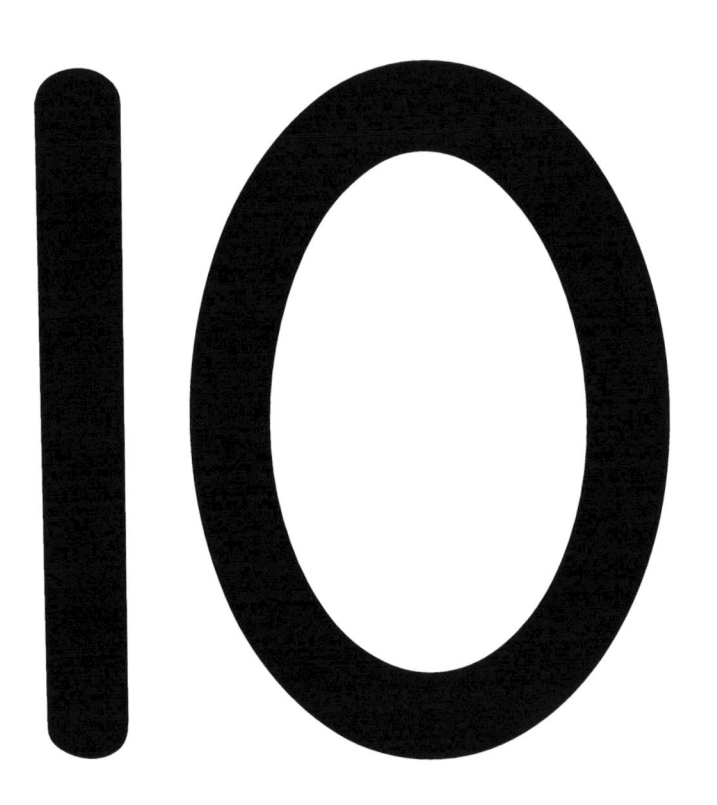

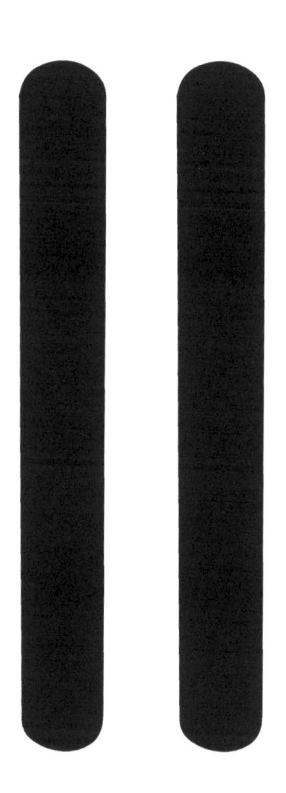

12

13

14

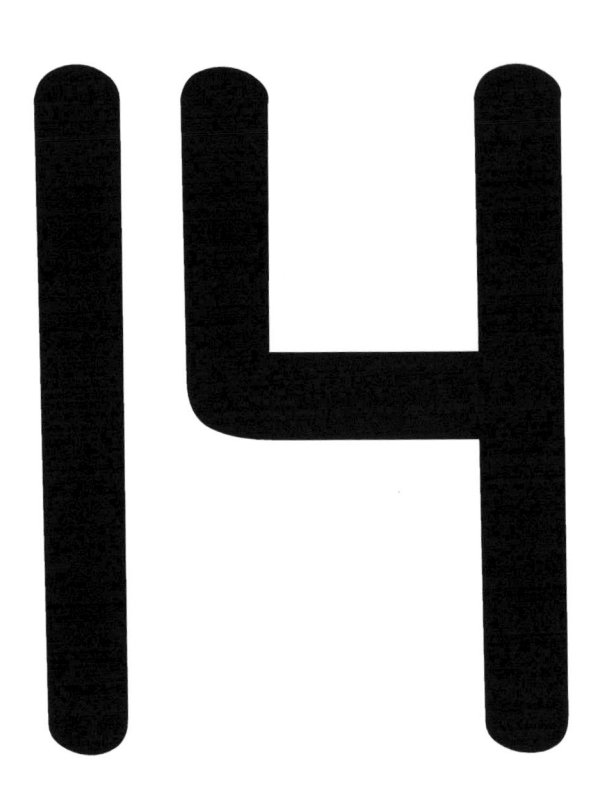

15

16

17

18

lq

20

Ten-frame Flash Cards 0-10

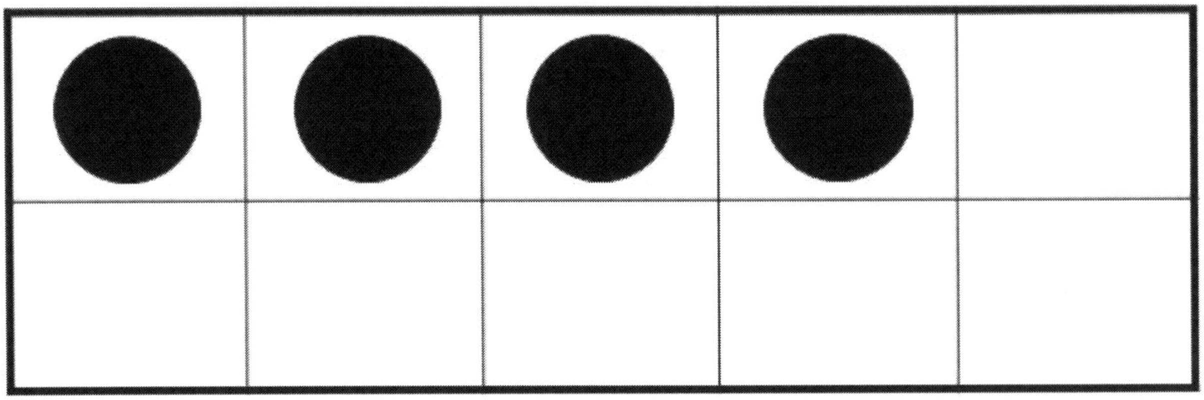

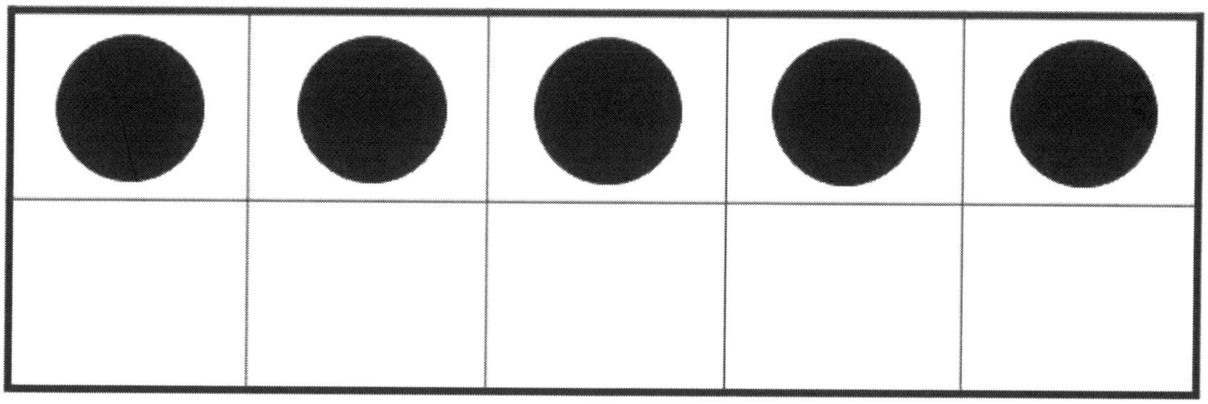

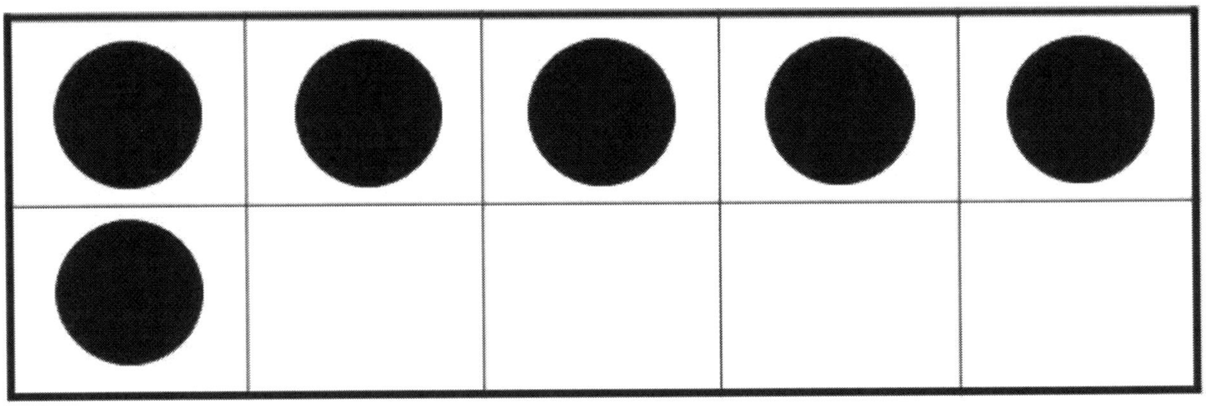

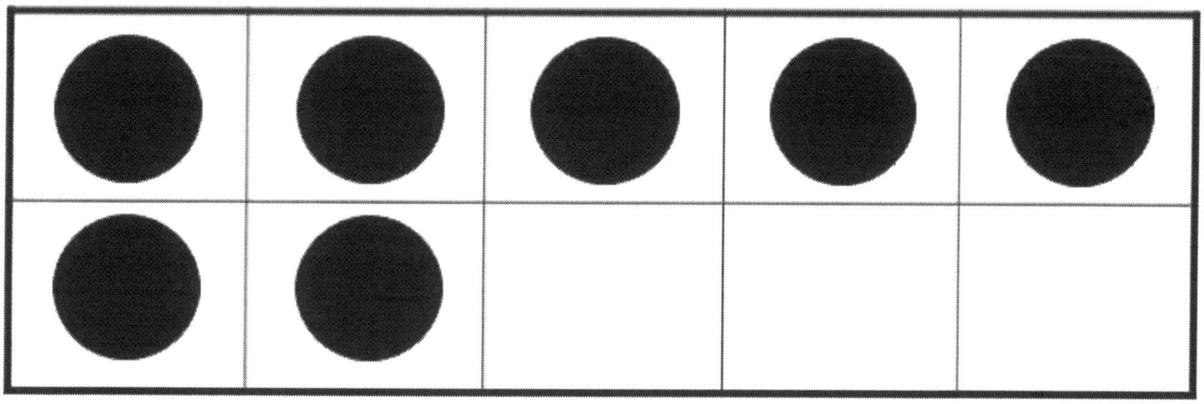

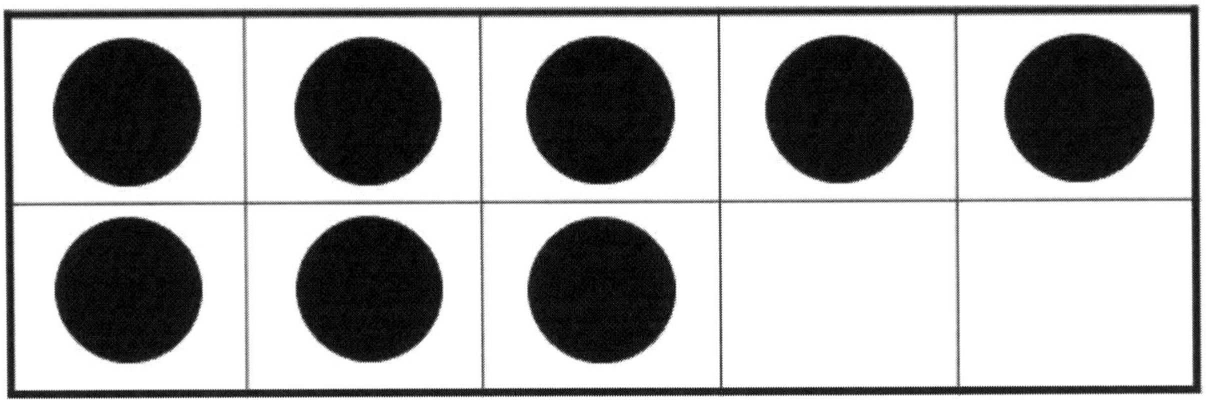

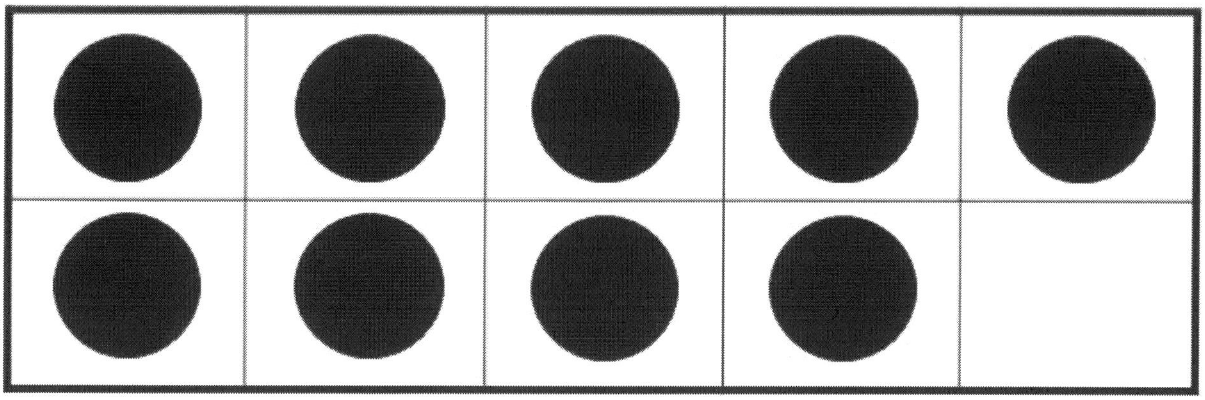

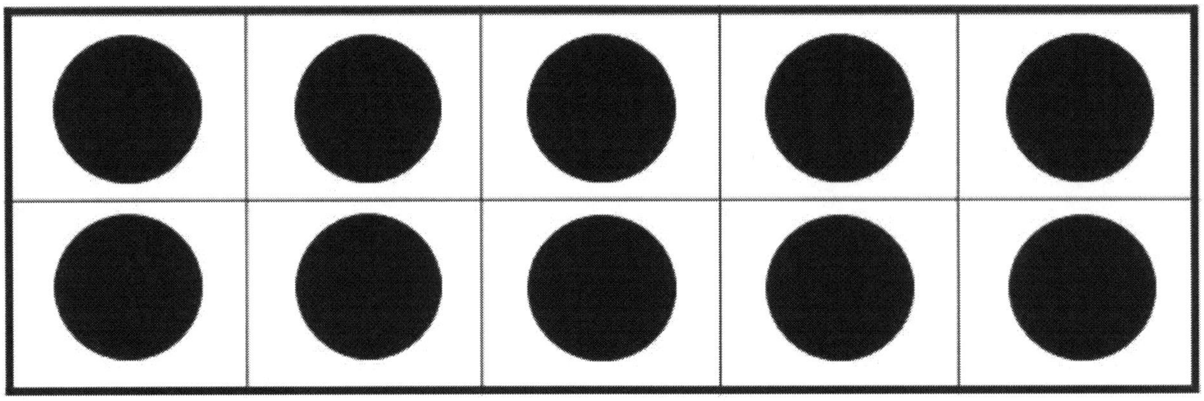

Ten-frame Flash Cards 0-10 Mixed-up

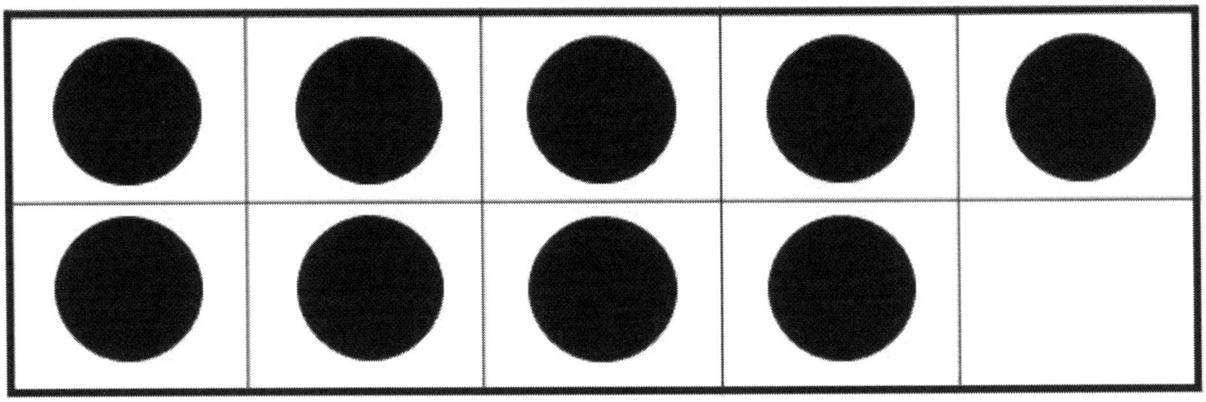

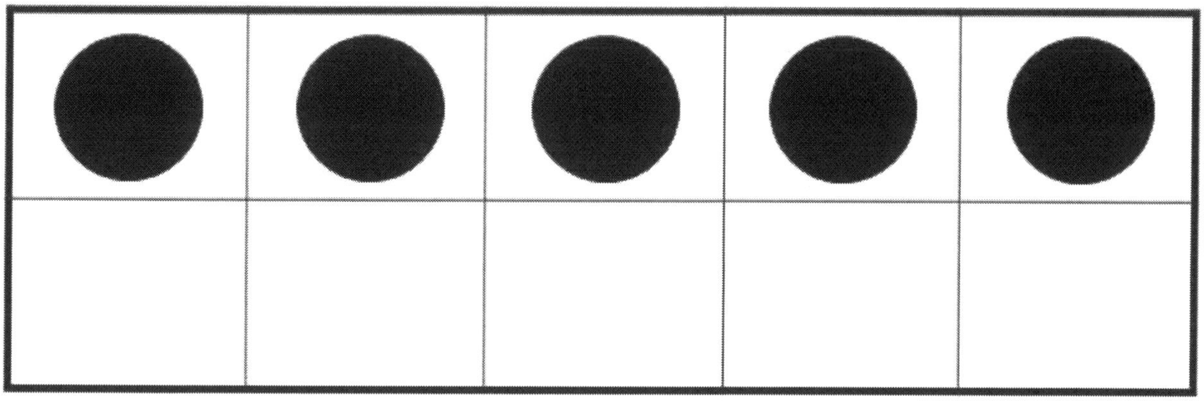

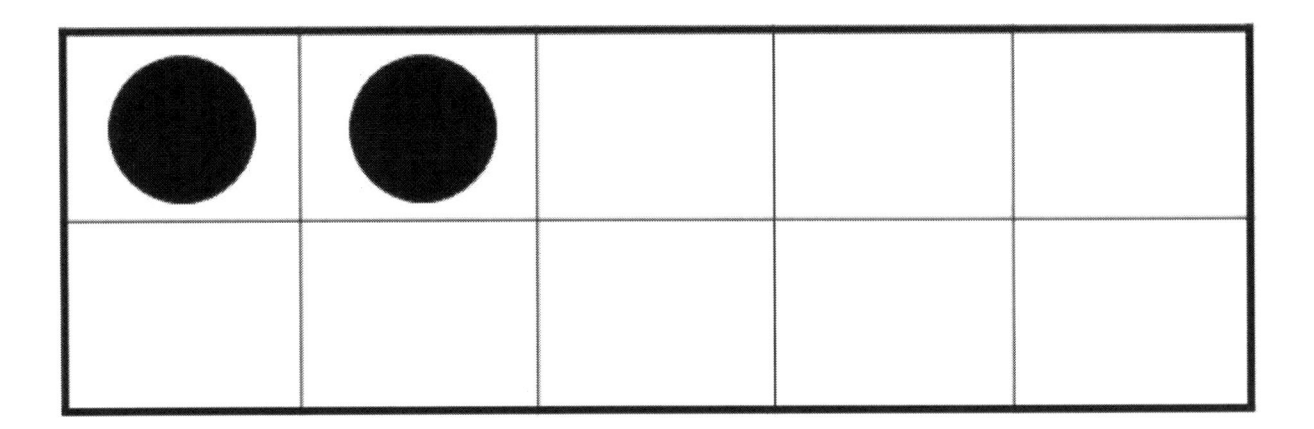

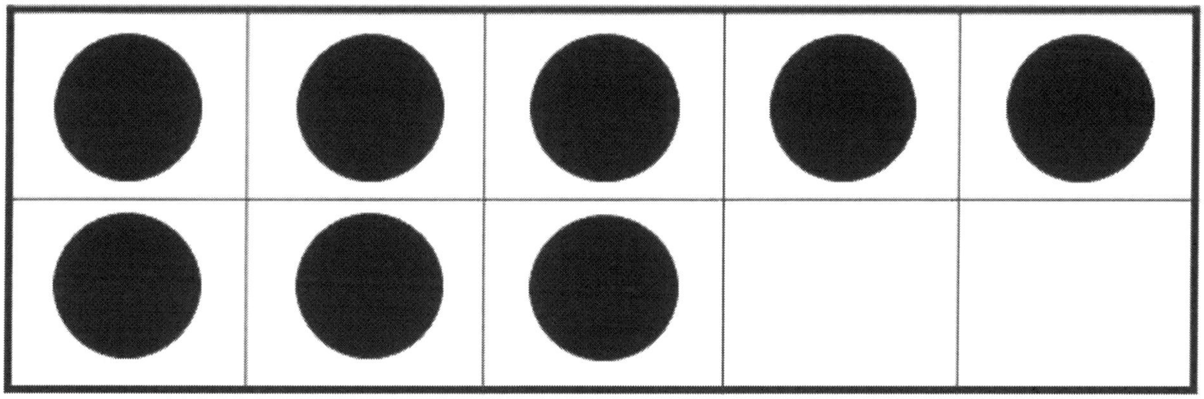

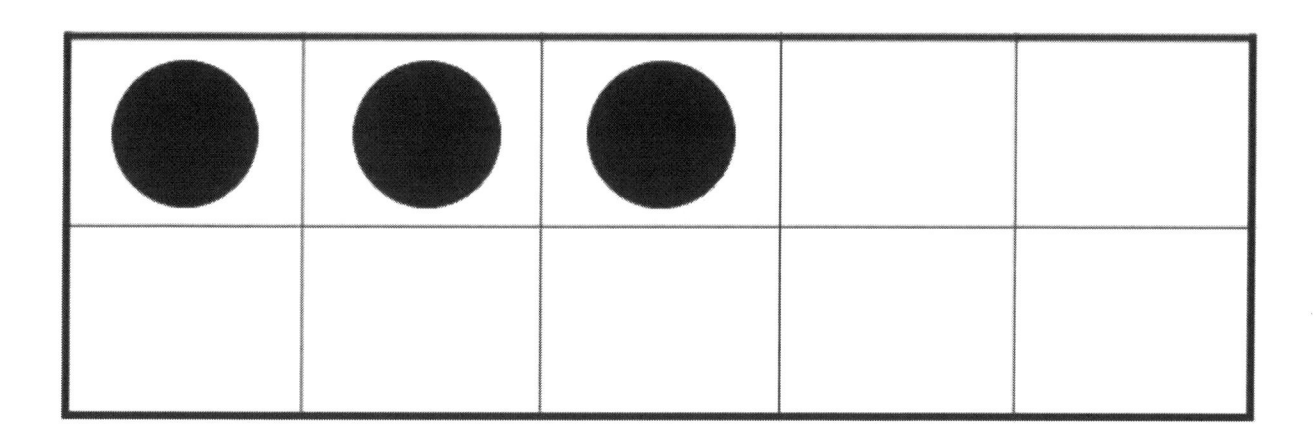

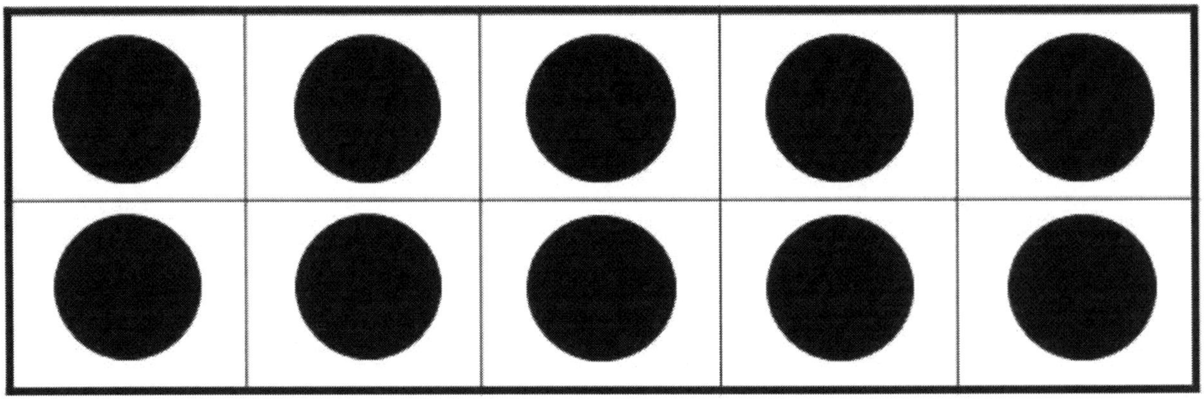

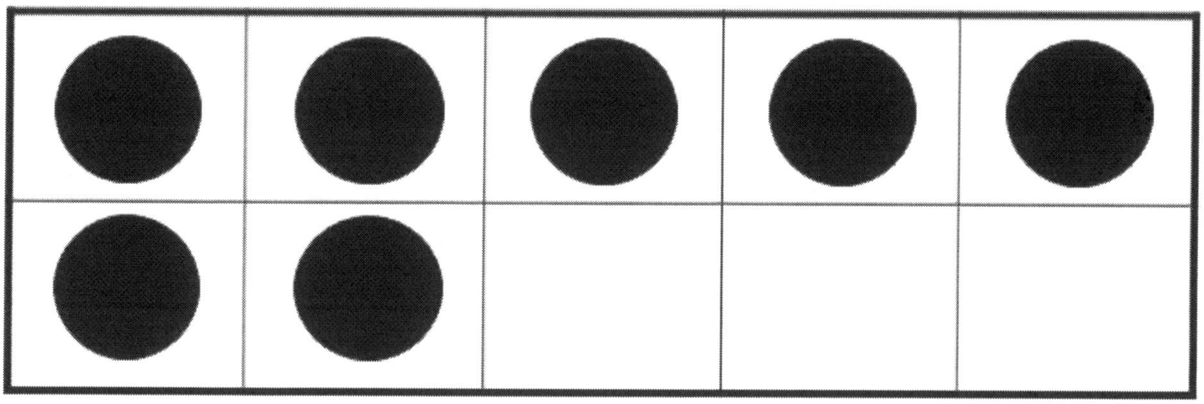

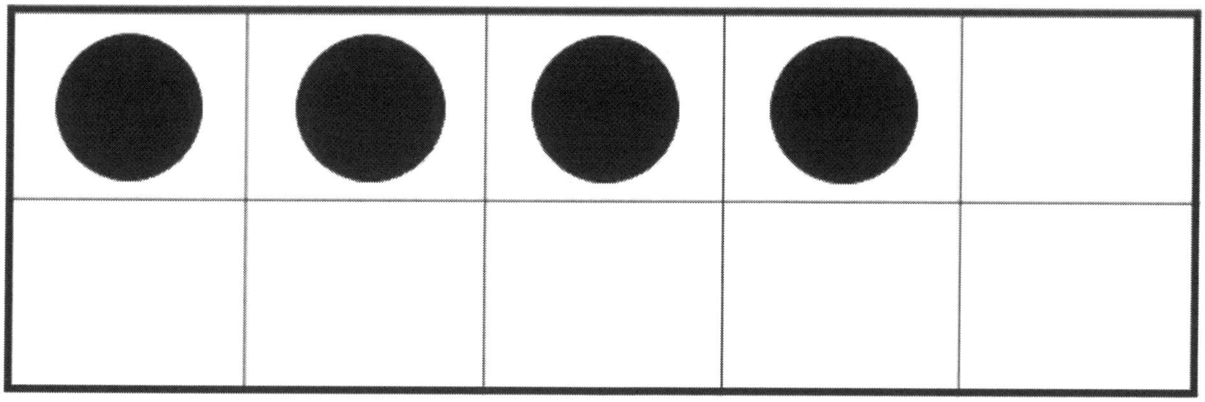

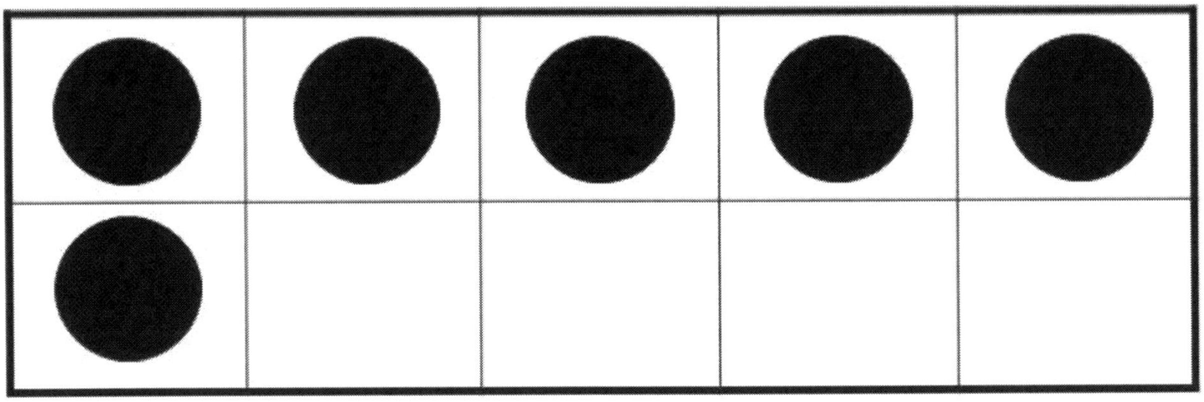

Ten-frame Flash Cards 11-20

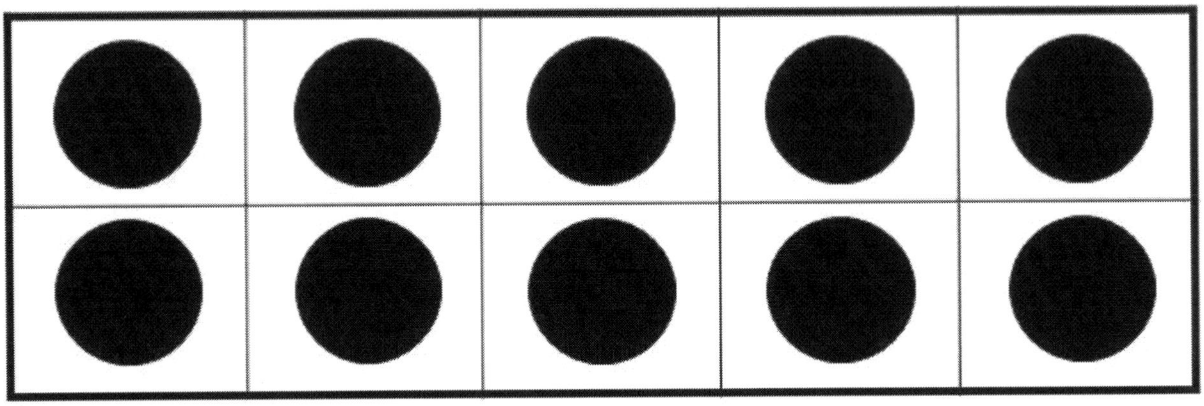

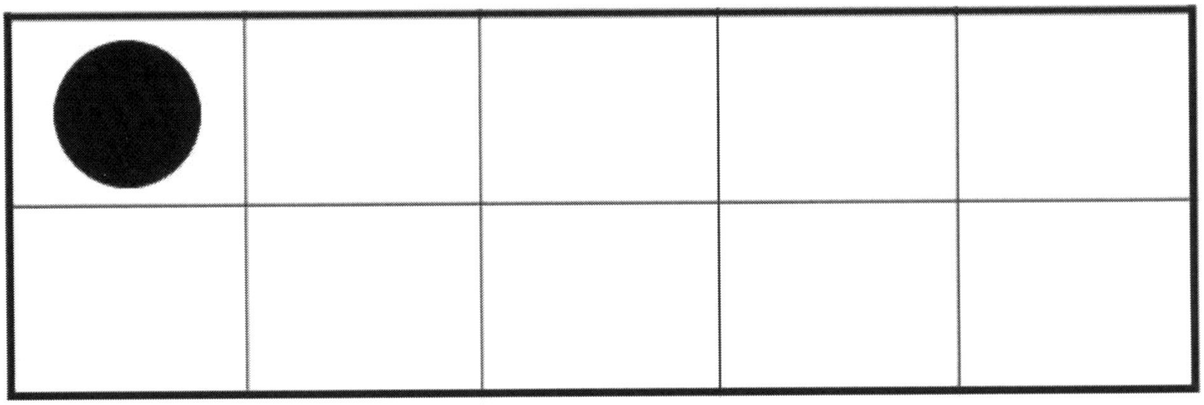

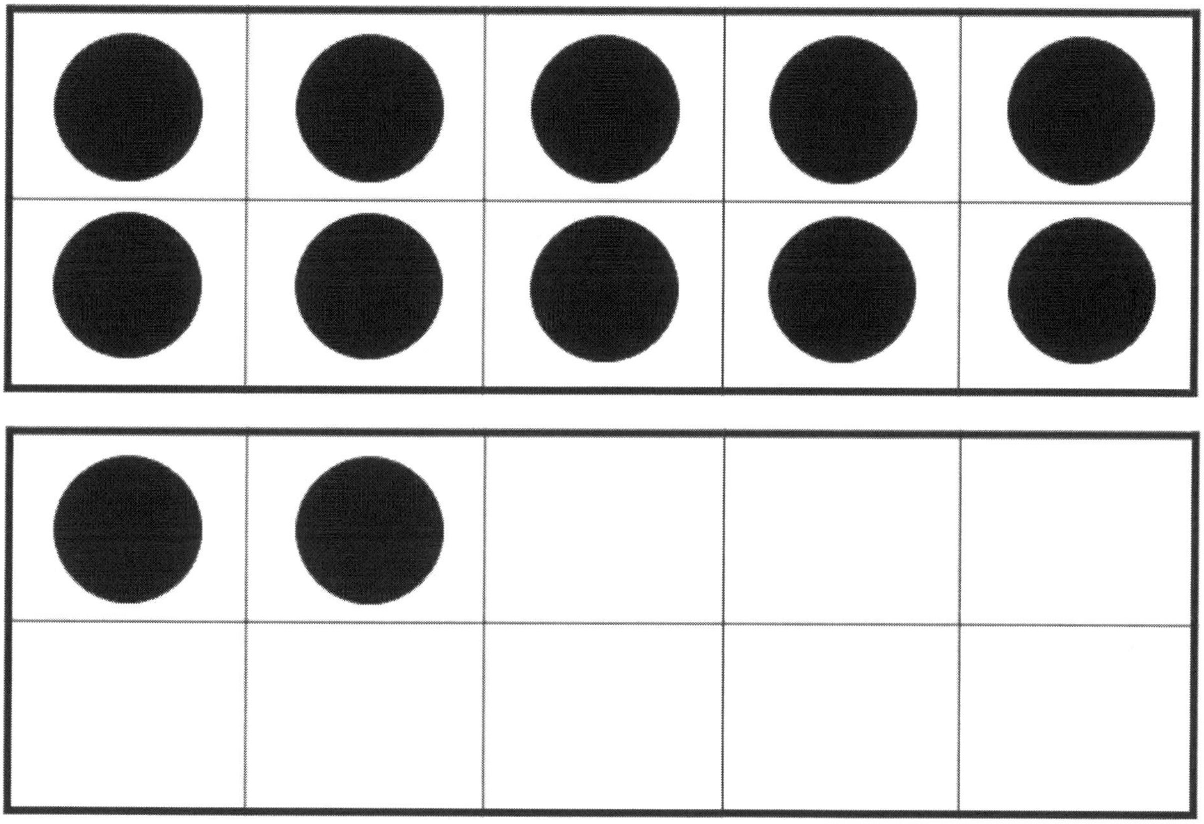

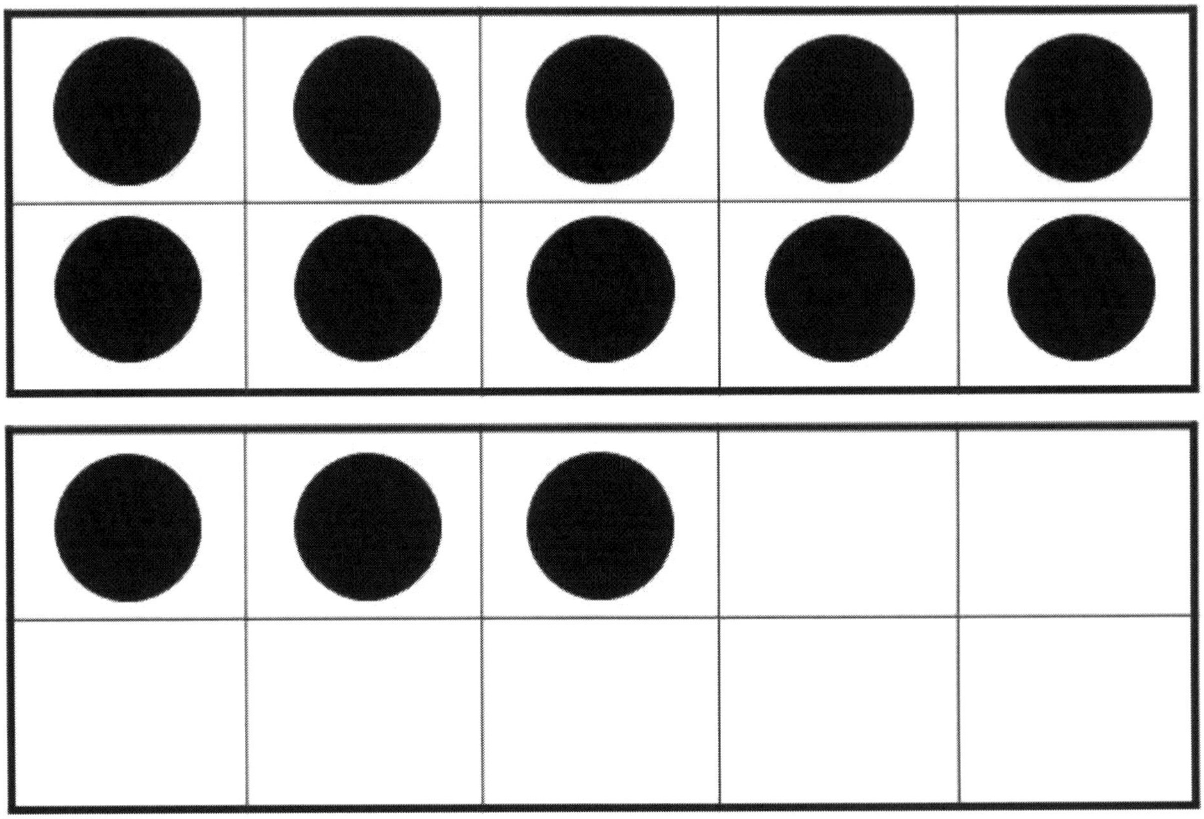

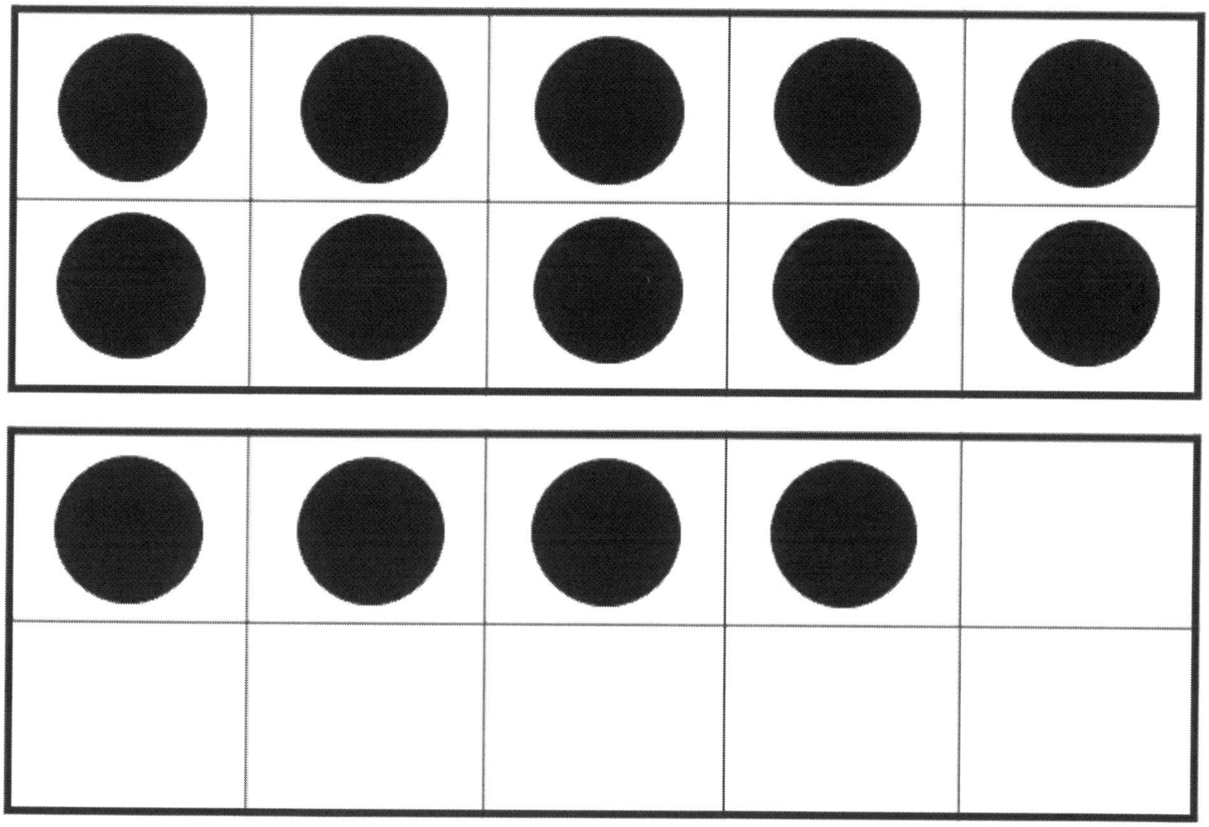

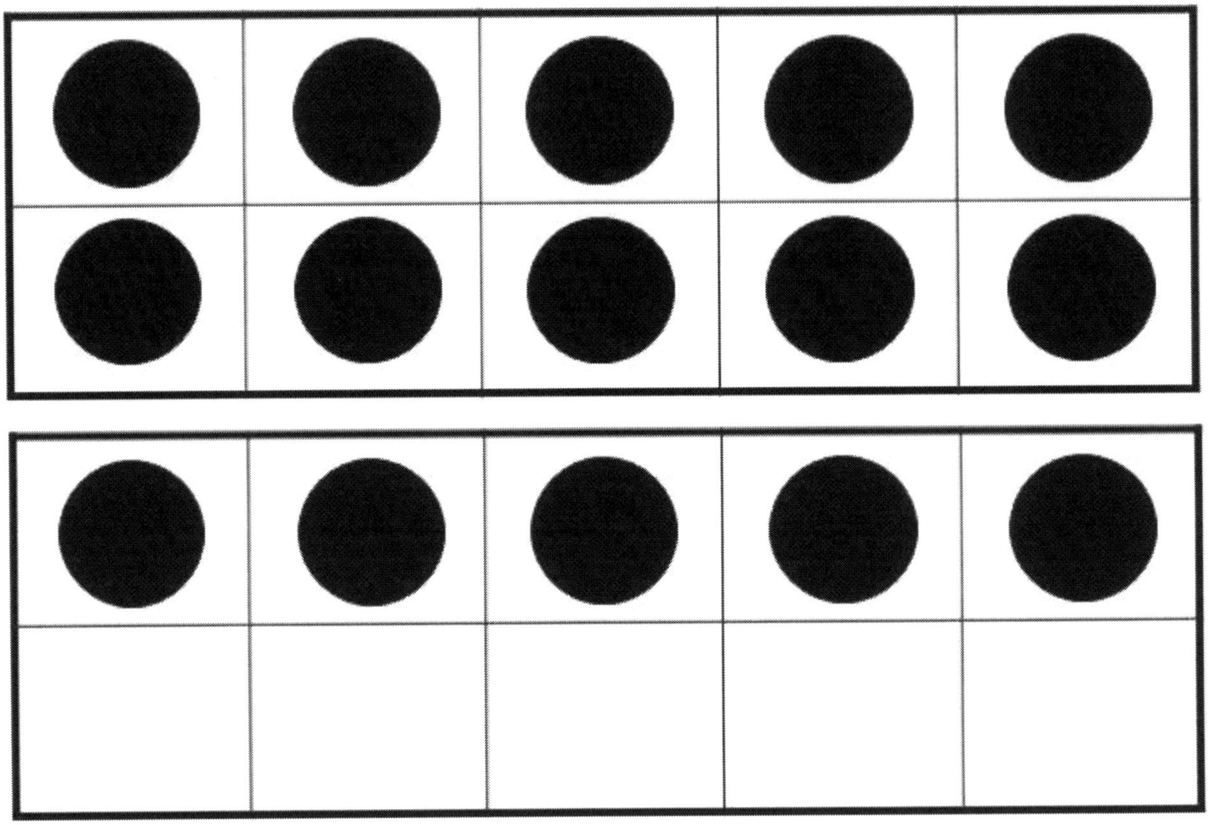

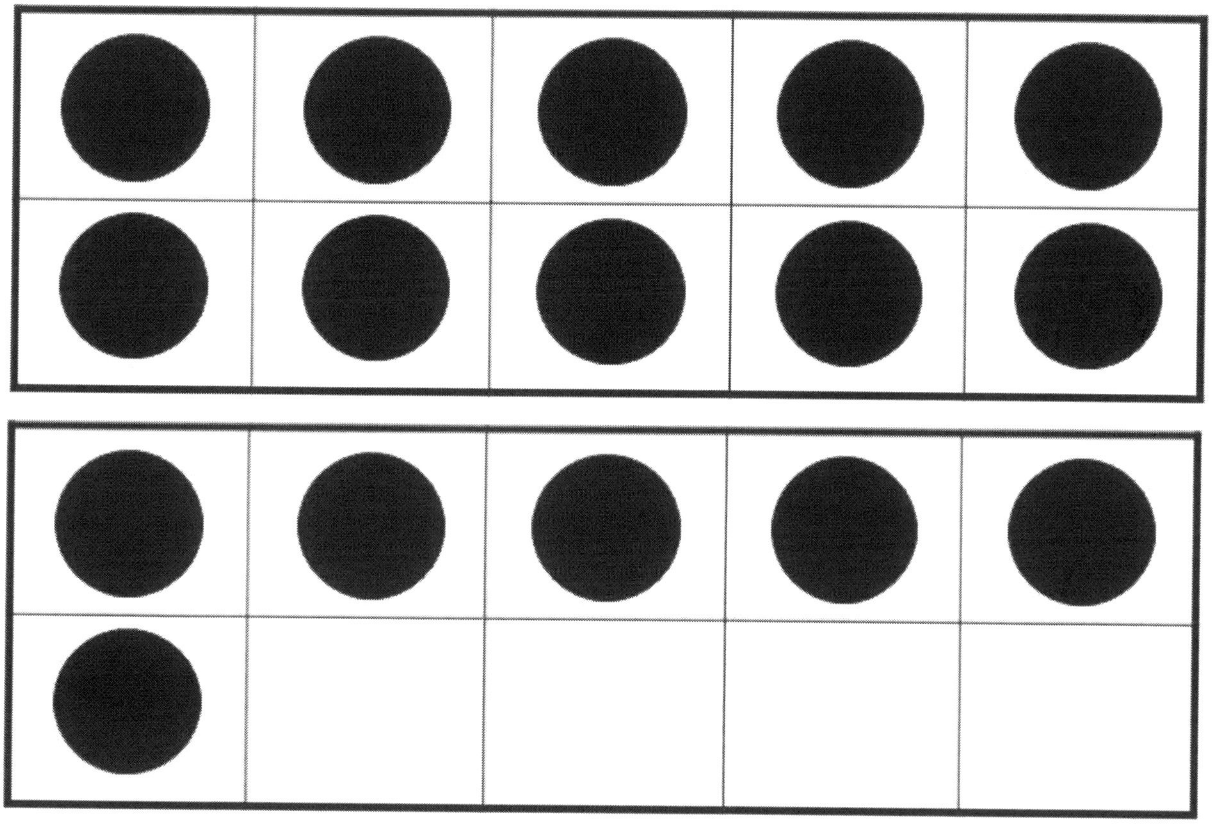

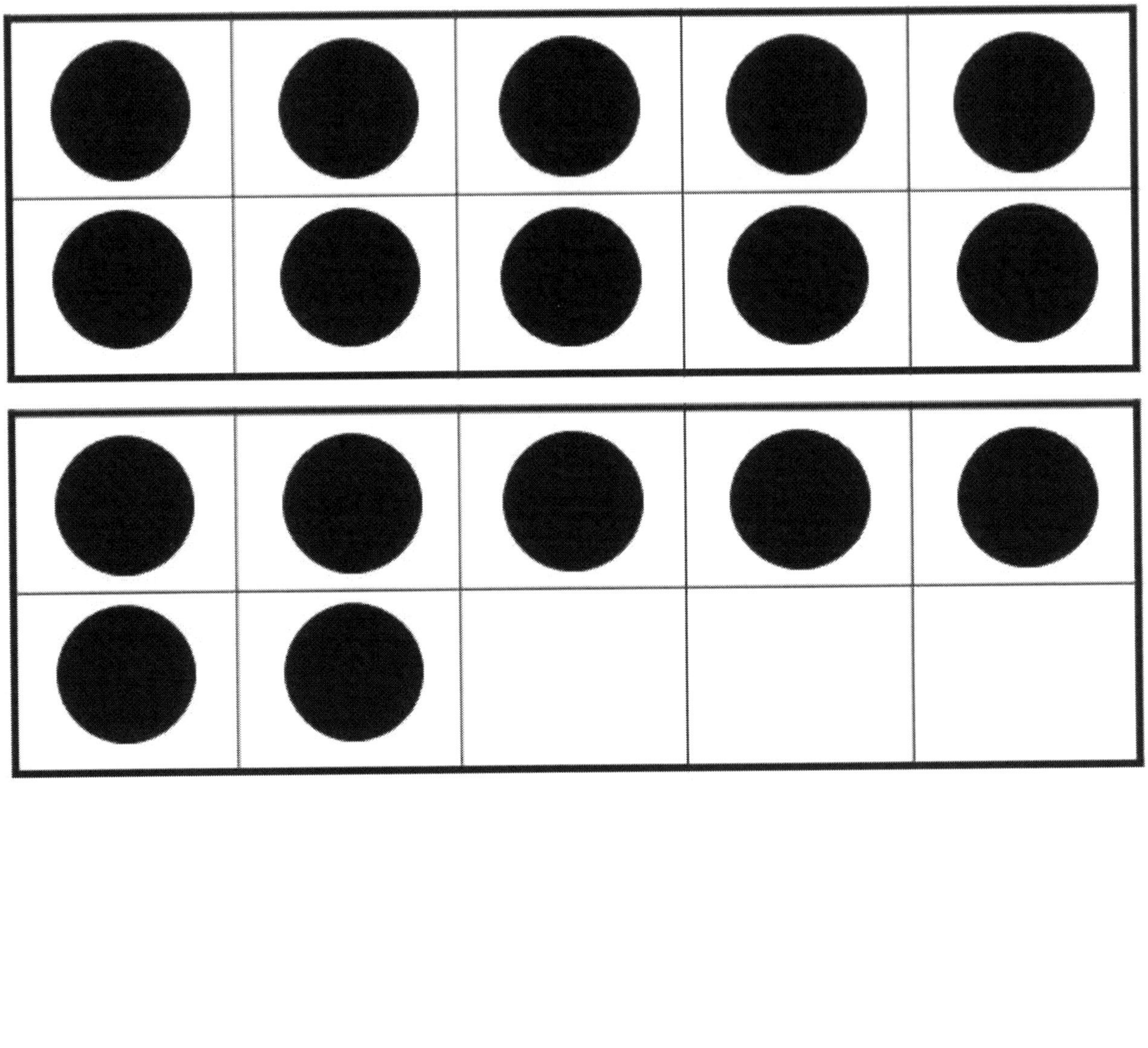

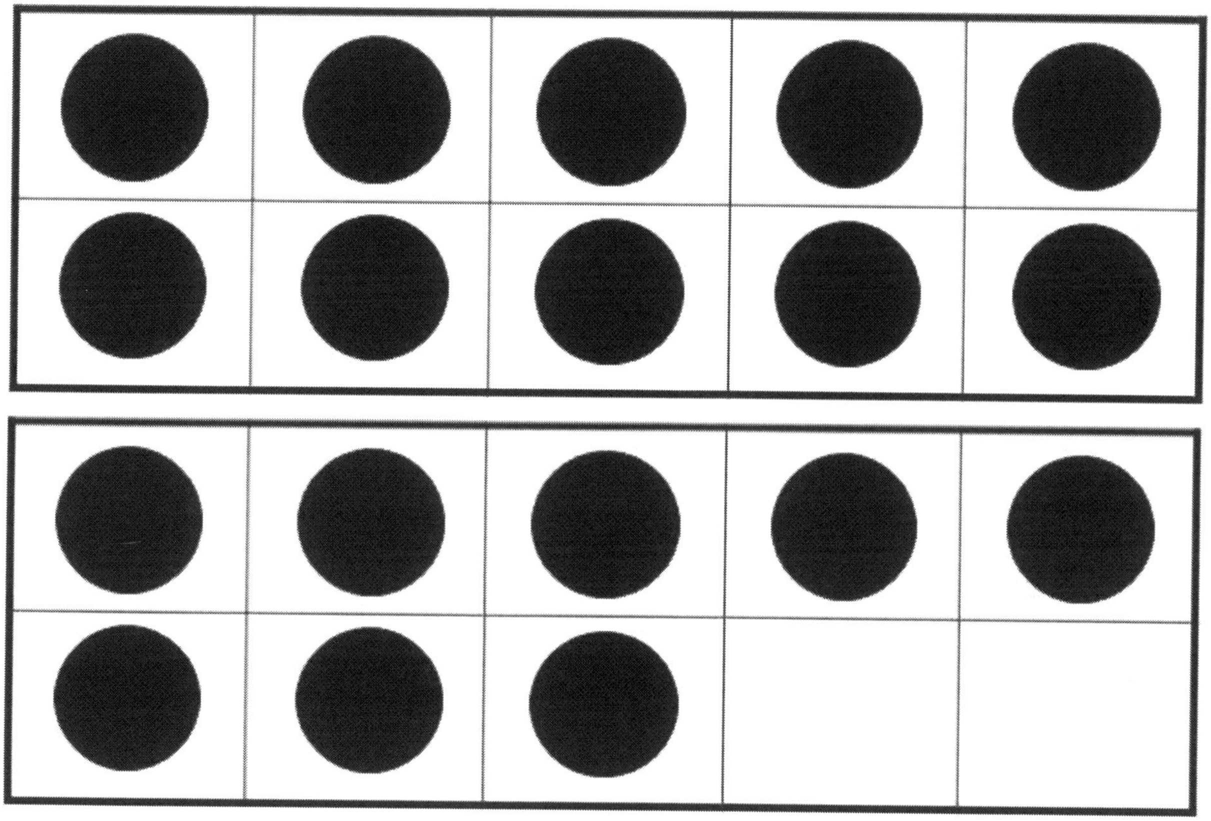

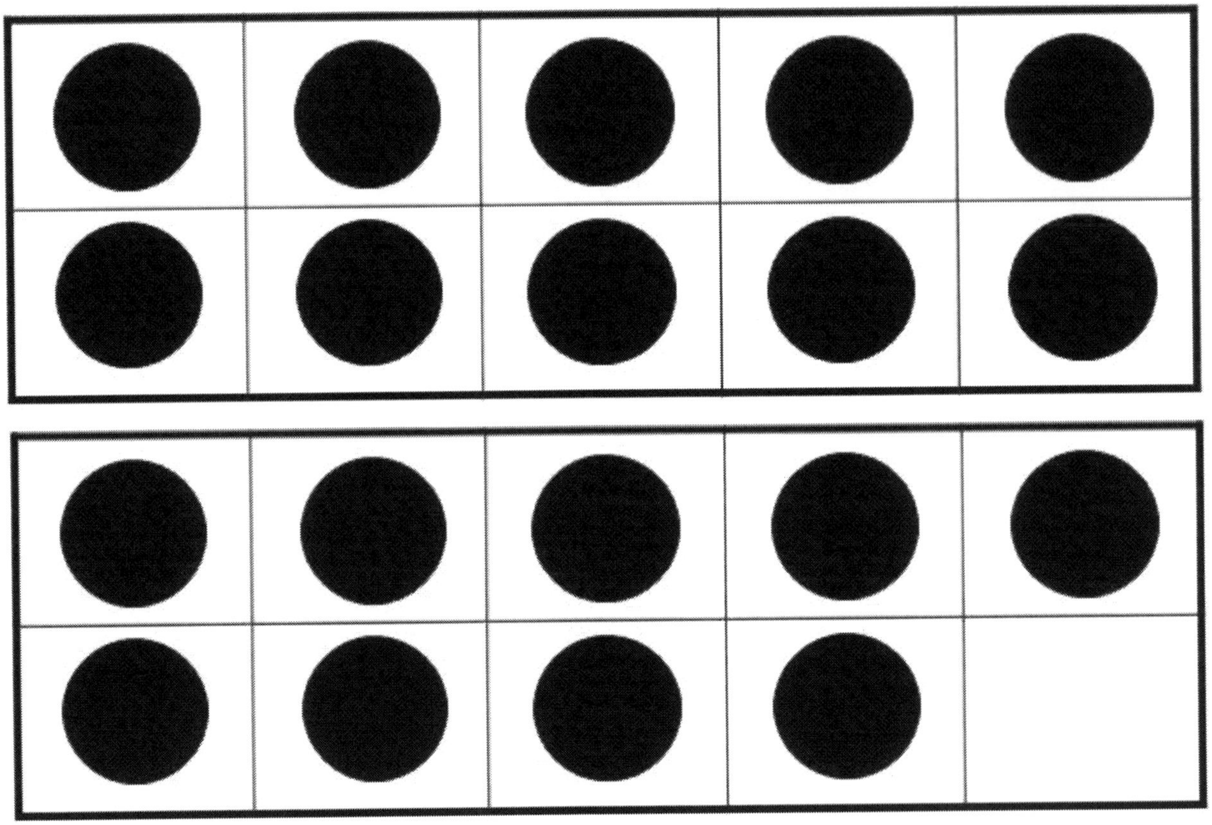

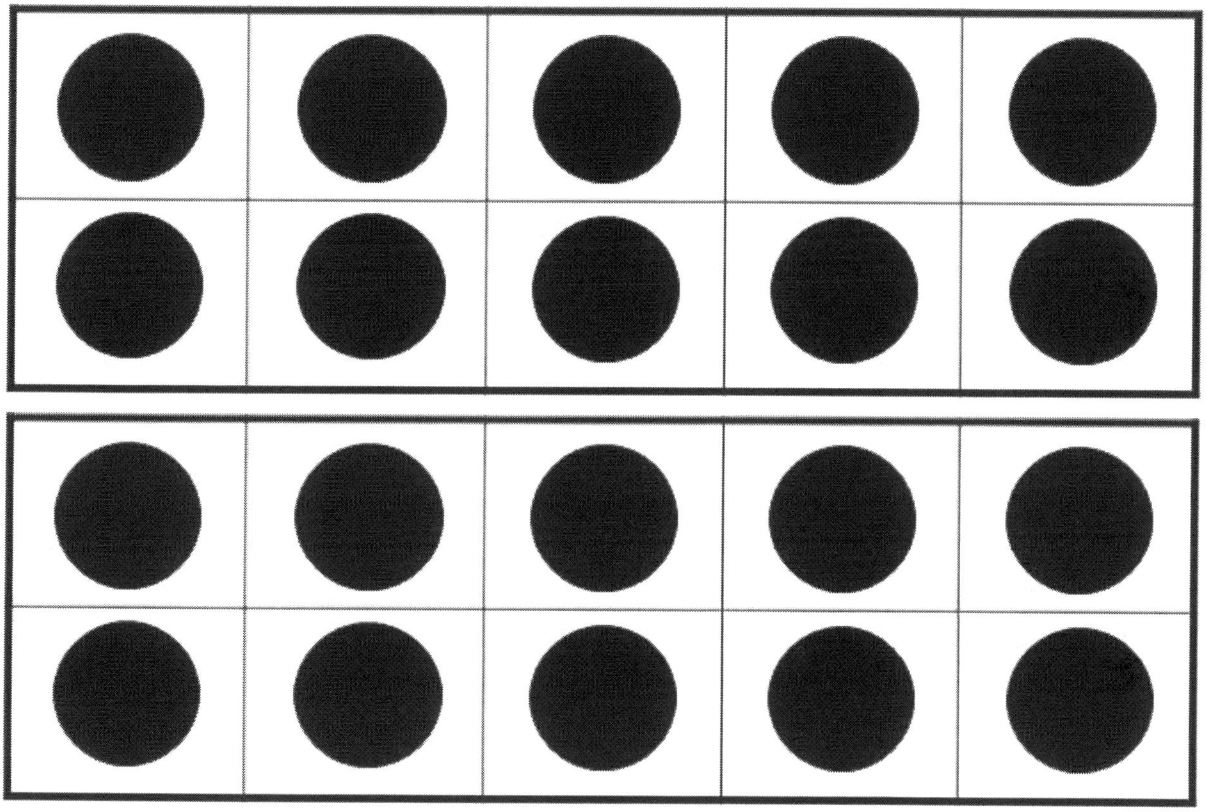

Ten-frame Flash Cards 11-20 Mixed-up

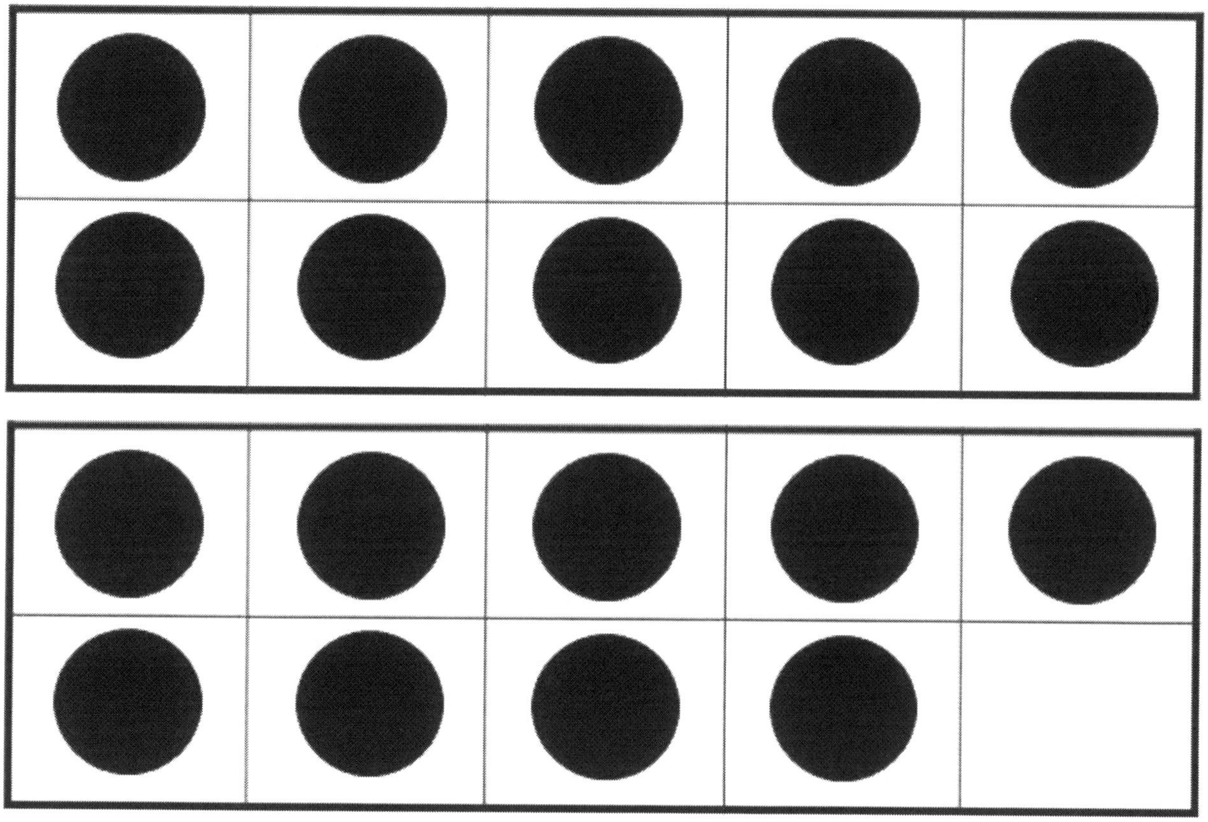

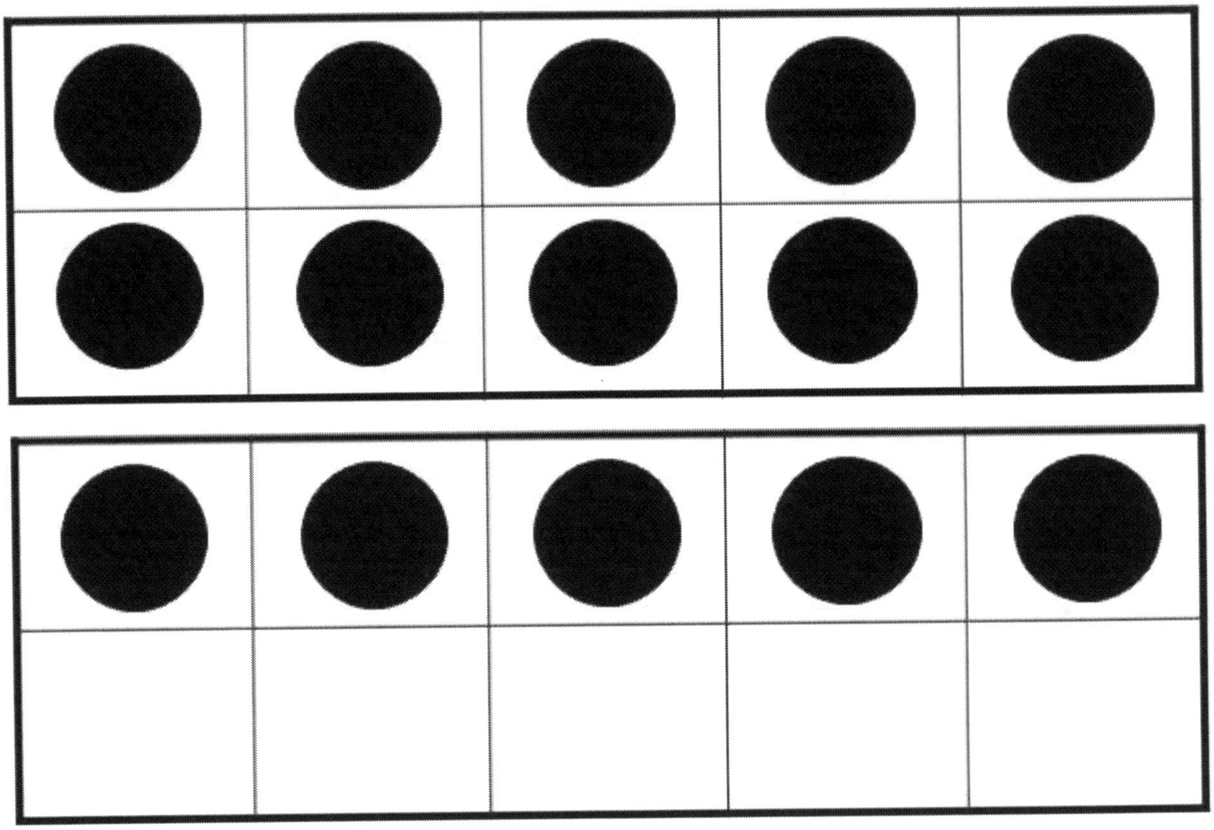

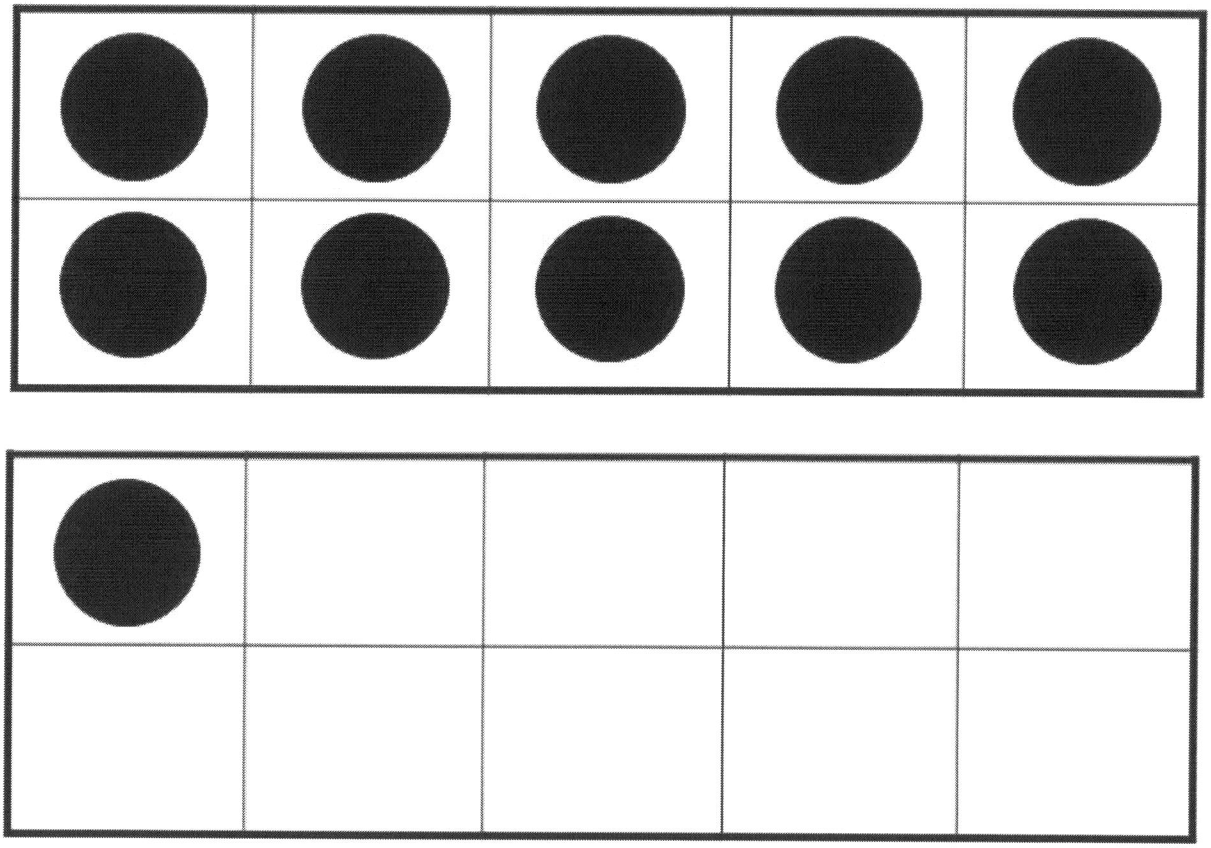

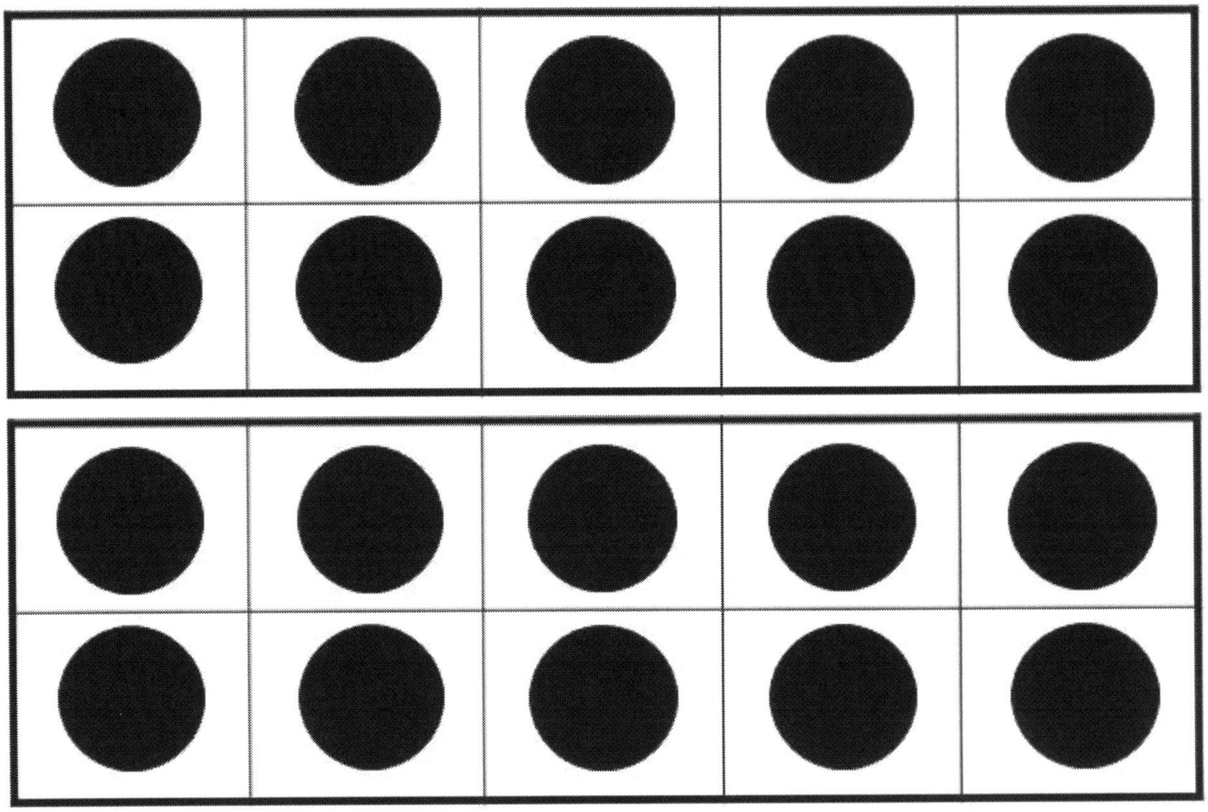

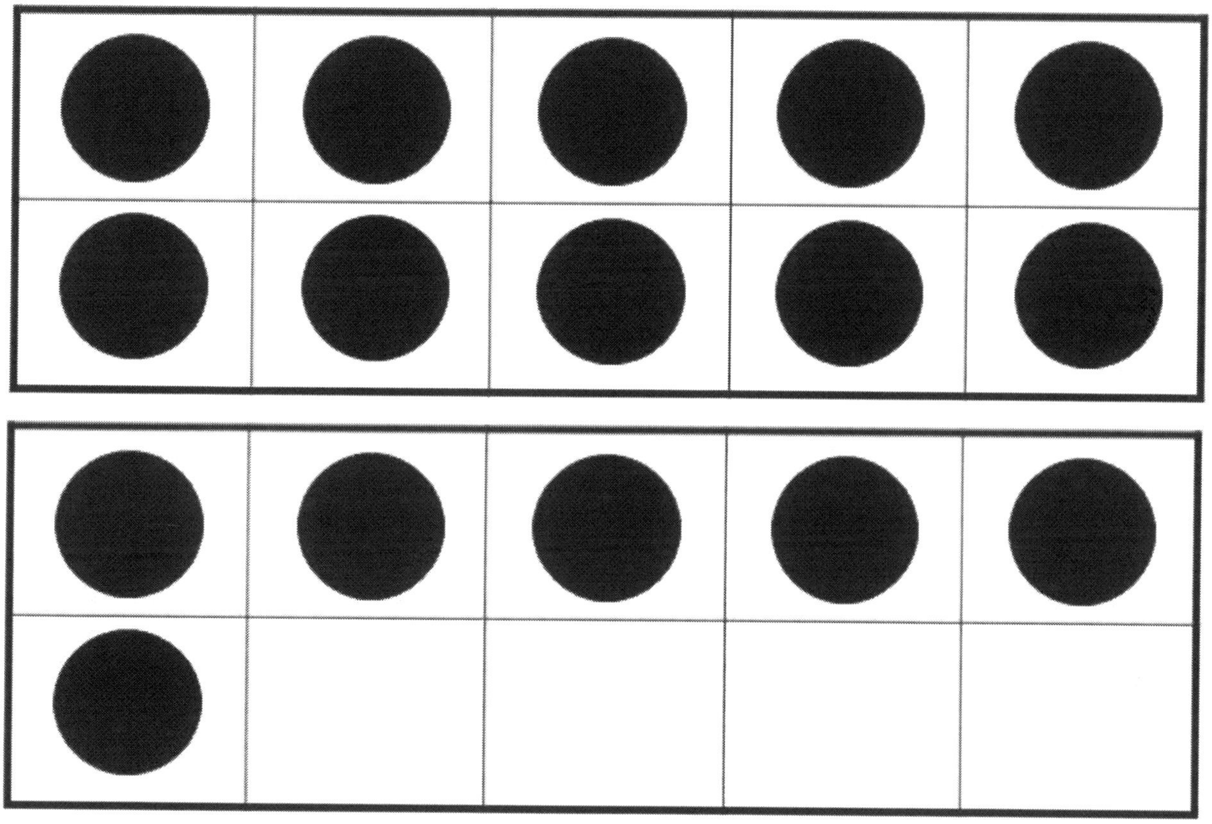

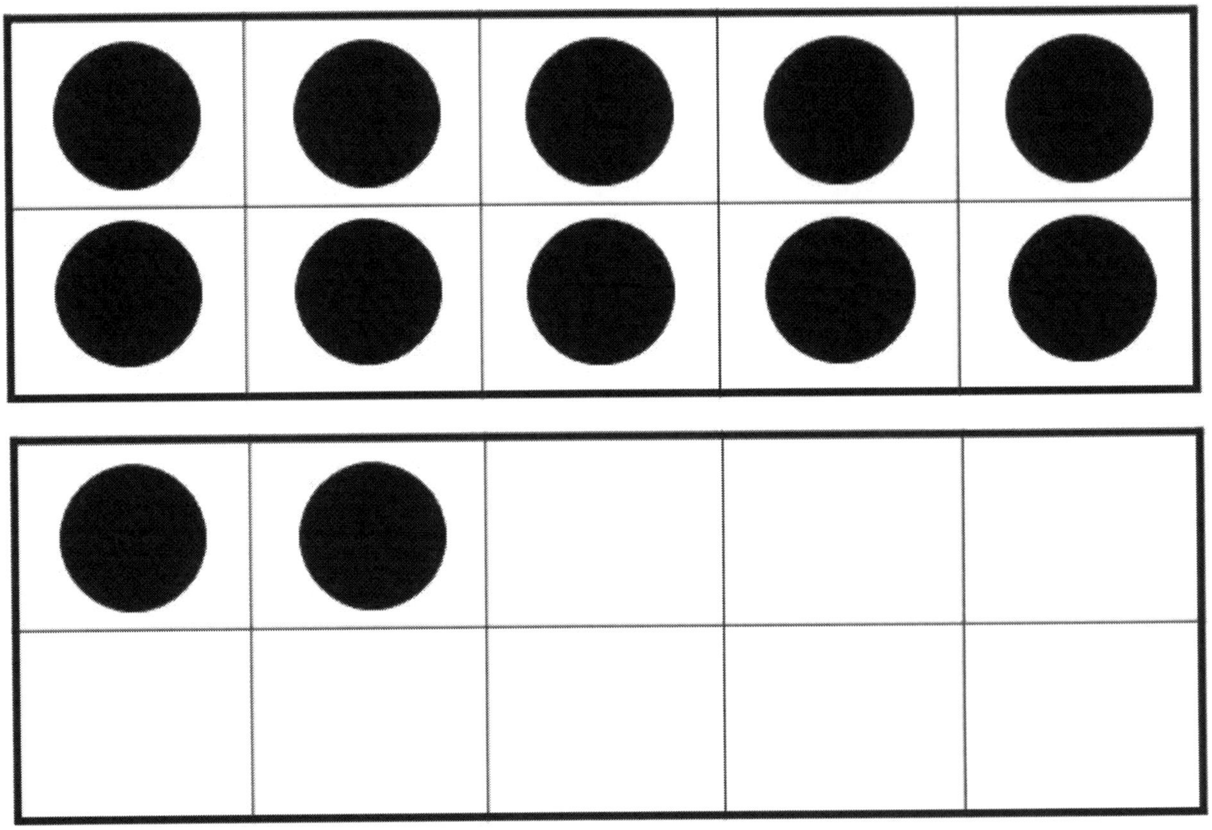

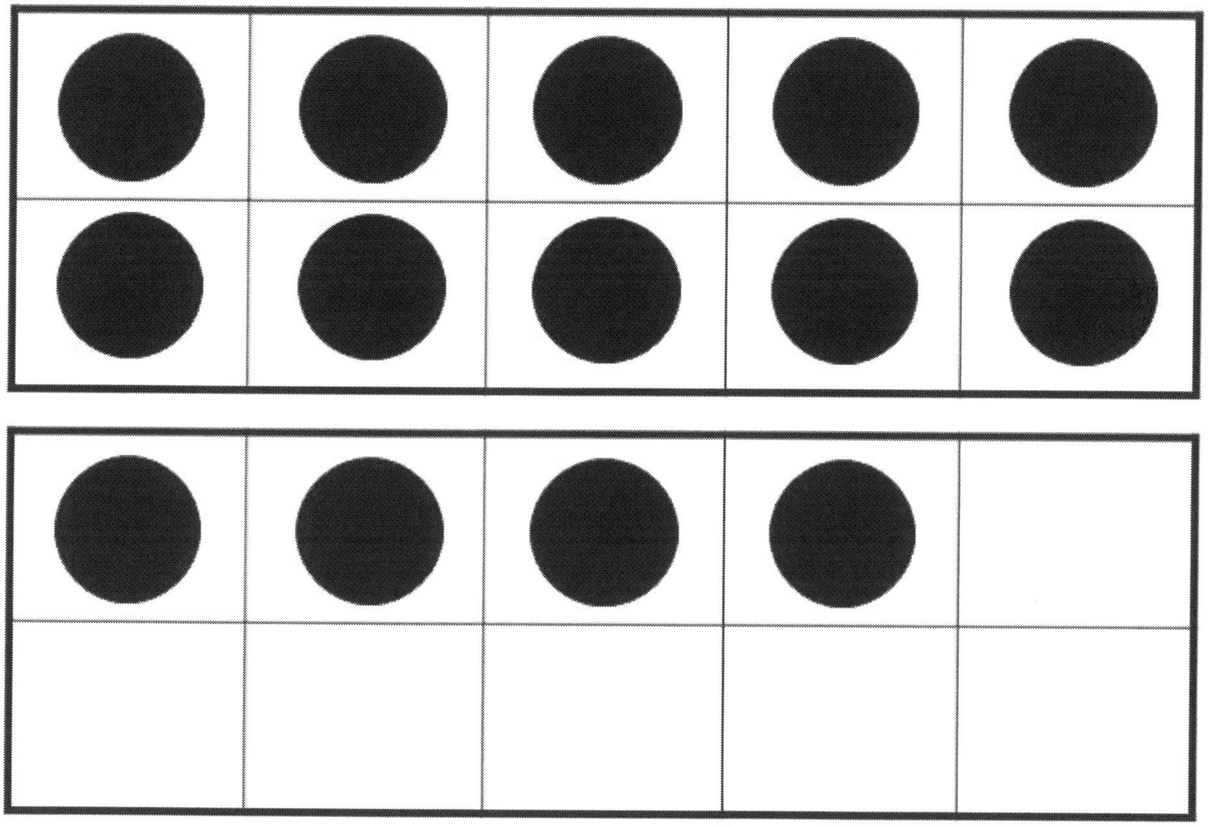

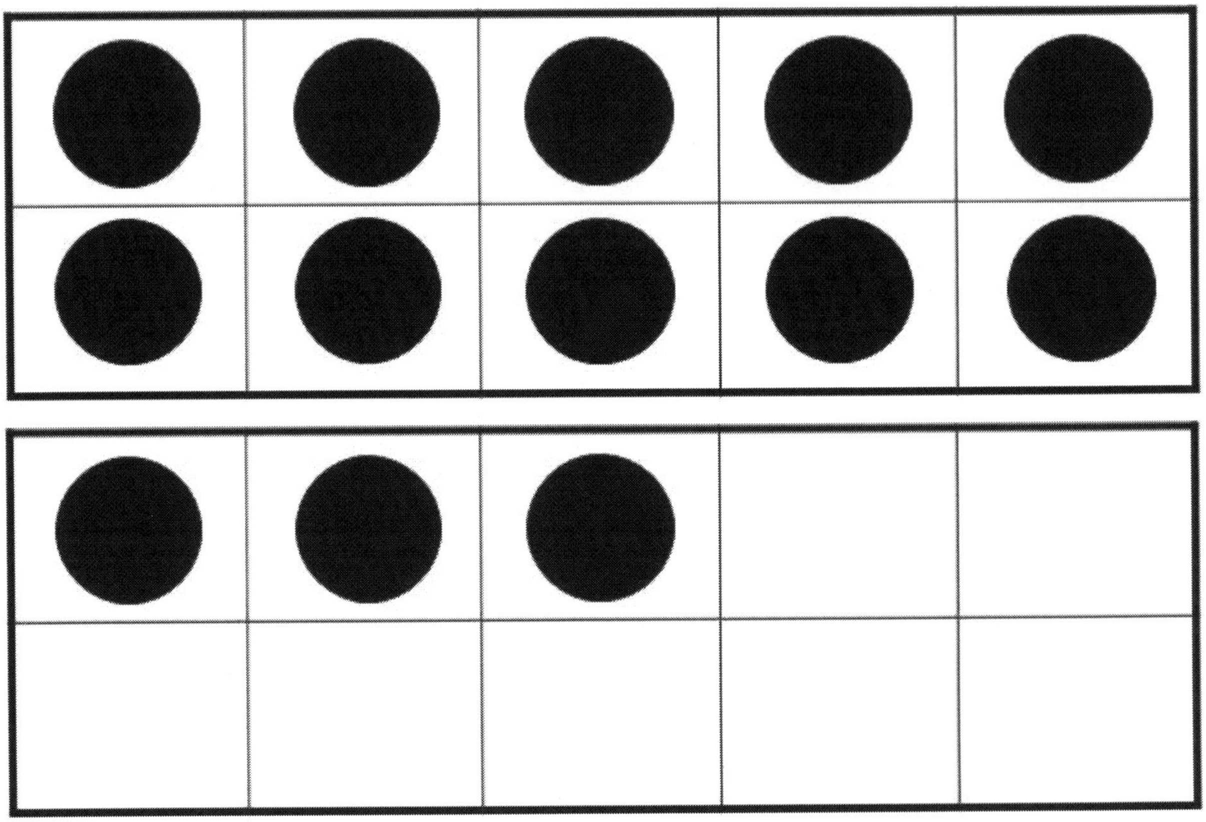

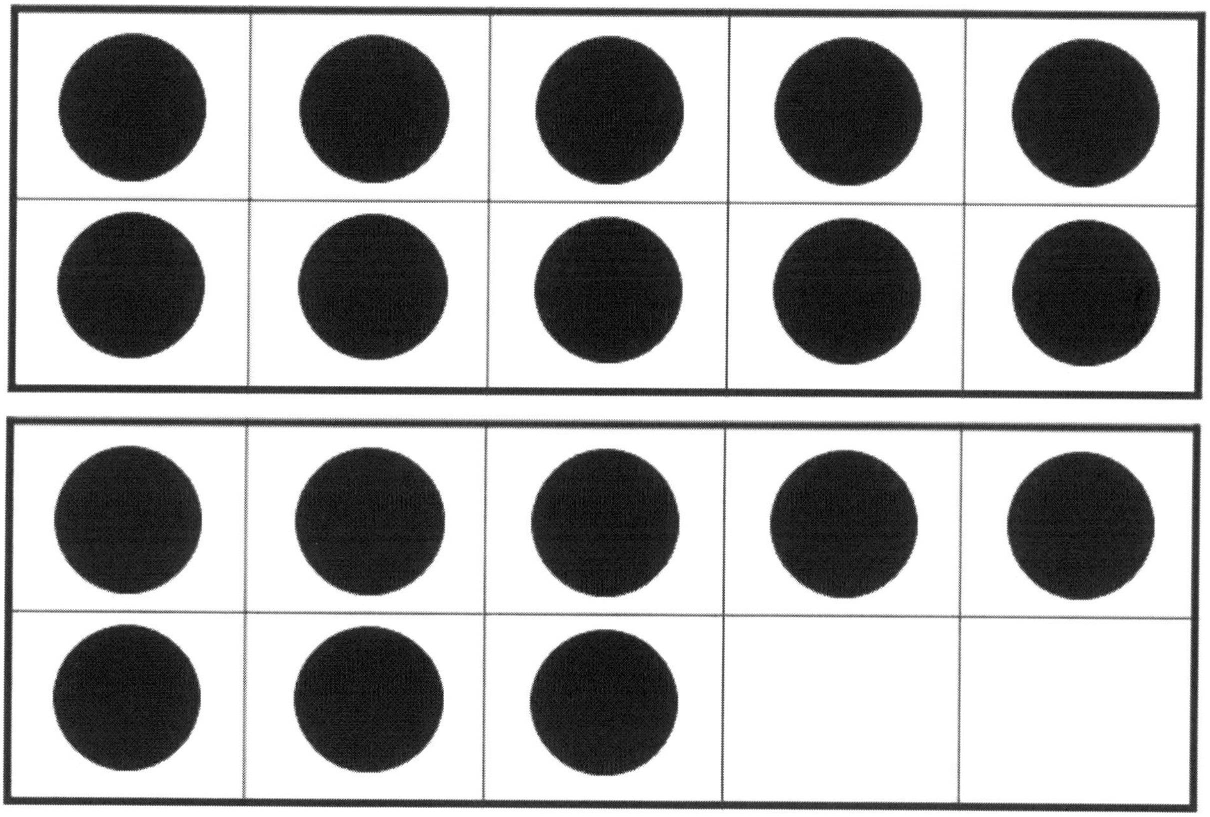

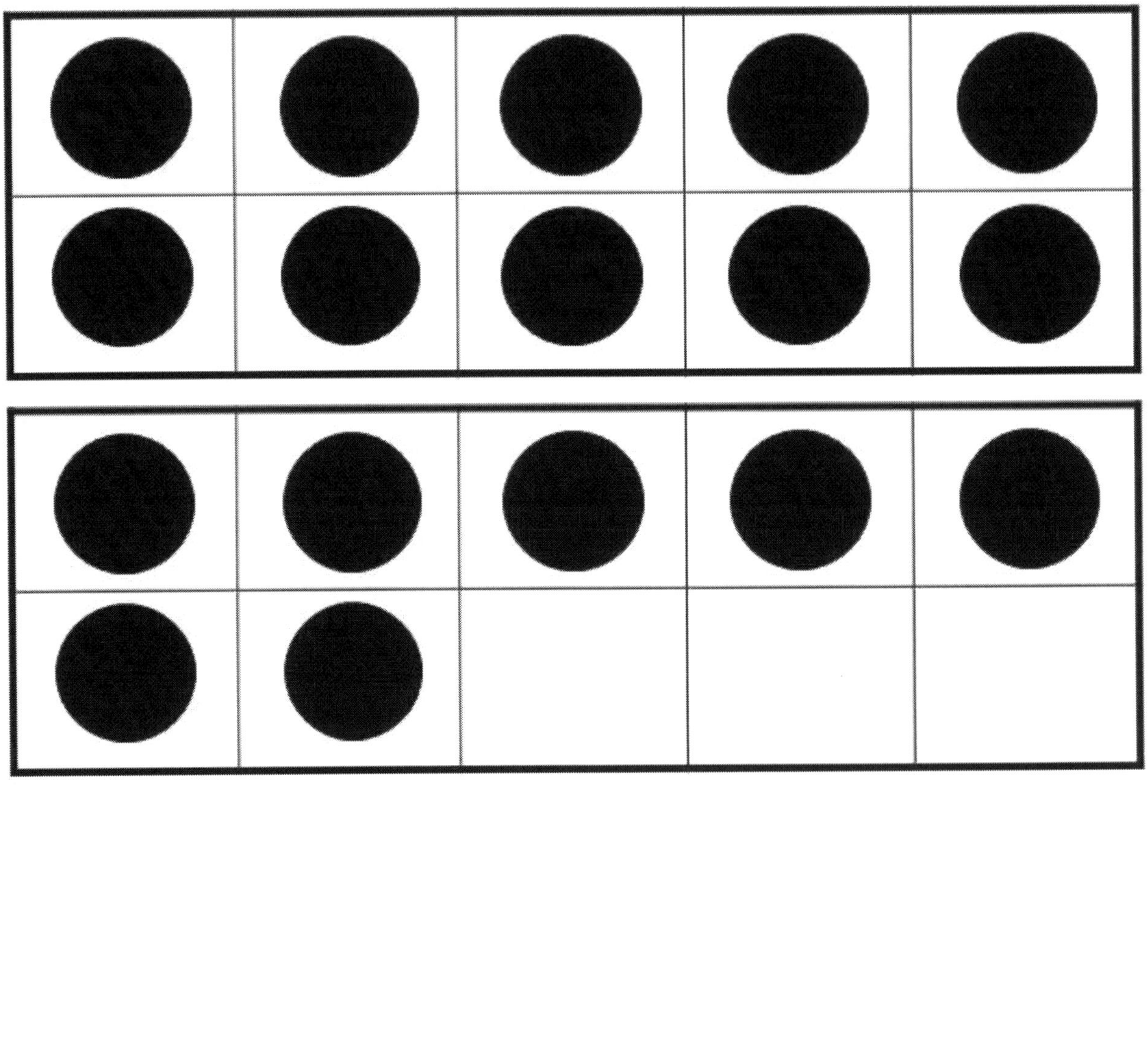

Printed in Great Britain
by Amazon